WEEKEND
FURNITURE PROJECTS

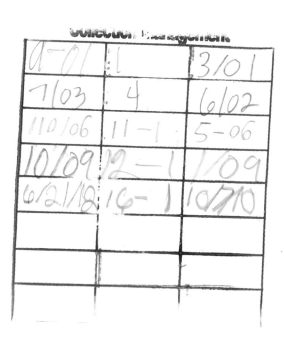

WEEKEND
FURNITURE PROJECTS

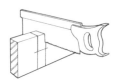

CHRIS SIMPSON

Hand Books Press

MADISON, WISCONSIN U.S.A.

Distributed by North Light Books
CINCINNATI, OHIO U.S.A.

Publisher's Acknowledgements

The publishers would like to thank Jason Waterhouse at Nice Irma's,
46 Goodge Street, London and Damask, 3–4 Broxholme House,
New Kings Road, London for lending props for photography and John
Boddy's Fine Wood and Tool Store Ltd, Riverside Sawmills,
Boroughbridge YO5 9LU for the wood photographs
on page 42.

Text and designs © Chris Simpson 1998
The moral right of the author has been asserted.
Photographs and illustrations © B T Batsford 1998

First published in 1999 by B T Batsford Ltd
Published in the U.S. by Hand Books Press
931 E. Main Street #106
Madison, W1 53703-2955

Distributed by North Light Books
An imprint of F&W Publications
1507 Dana Avenue
Cincinnati, OH 45207
TEL 800-289-0963 FAX 513-531-4082

684.1042   ISBN 0-9658248-7-X

Printed in Hong Kong

Photography of pages 37, 51, 69, 77, 109 & 119 by Paul Bricknell
and of pages 21, 29, 59, 85, 91 & 101 by Ben Jennings
Illustrations by Peter Gerrish
Designed by DWN, London

CONTENTS

Introduction   7

CHAPTER 1

Equipment and Basic Preparation   9

Equipment   10

Basic Preparation   14

CHAPTER 2

The Projects: 19

Mirror/Picture Frame   20

Occasional Table   28

Solid Timber   31

Adhesives   32

Bookcase   36

Choosing Timber   41

Sharpening Edge Tools   43

Abrasives   45

Magazine Rack   50

Colour, Pattern and Texture   53

Wall-hung Cabinet   58

TV and Video Unit   68

Manufactured Board   72

Hi-fi Unit   76

Finishing   78

Drop-leaf Table   84

Corner Cupboard   92

Veneer   95

Sewing Box   100

Display Cabinet   108

Fittings   112

Settle   118

List of Suppliers   127

Index   128

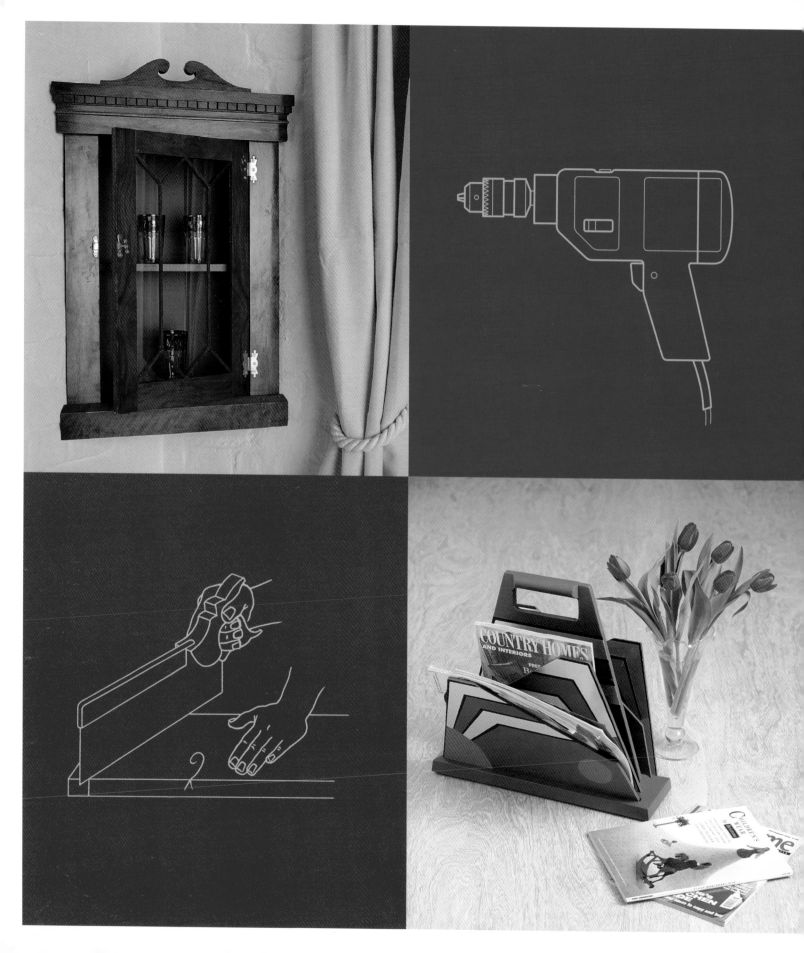

INTRODUCTION

THE PURPOSE OF THIS BOOK is to help you make attractive and practical pieces of furniture for the living room with relative ease. Obviously, not everyone will have the same level of skill. You may be a novice or an expert or somewhere in between. I aim to show you the general processes involved in making each piece as clearly and simply as possible. Each project identifies the main material used, whether it is solid timber or manufactured board, and offers advice on selection and purchase, taking you through the stages of preparation, cutting, surfacing, final assembly, finishing and applying fittings.

Your experience may be in hand-making or in using mainly power or machine tools. The projects are all specially selected to enable you to make the best use of the skills and tools you have, however basic or sophisticated they may be, and to develop ways of construction that are most suited to your own way of working. Some people will be fairly didactic and say there is only one correct way of undertaking a particular process. However, I believe that there are many ways of achieving an end, all valid within the context of the person and the piece. Thus you will find that in many cases in this book at least one alternative way of carrying out a particular process is suggested.

When making furniture it is important that it should suit both the surroundings and the owner's personal taste. Therefore the book gives a range of options so that you can adapt the piece to your own needs and preferences. The construction of these options is basically the same as the project that has been photographed, but they differ in terms of materials used, the addition of extra details, in their types of closures and finishes. I have chosen four styles: country, reproduction, modern and designer. One of these is made up and photographed for each project, while the three alternatives are covered by notes and illustrations.

I wish you many happy hours making furniture and hope that the results will bring pleasure both to you and to the recipients.

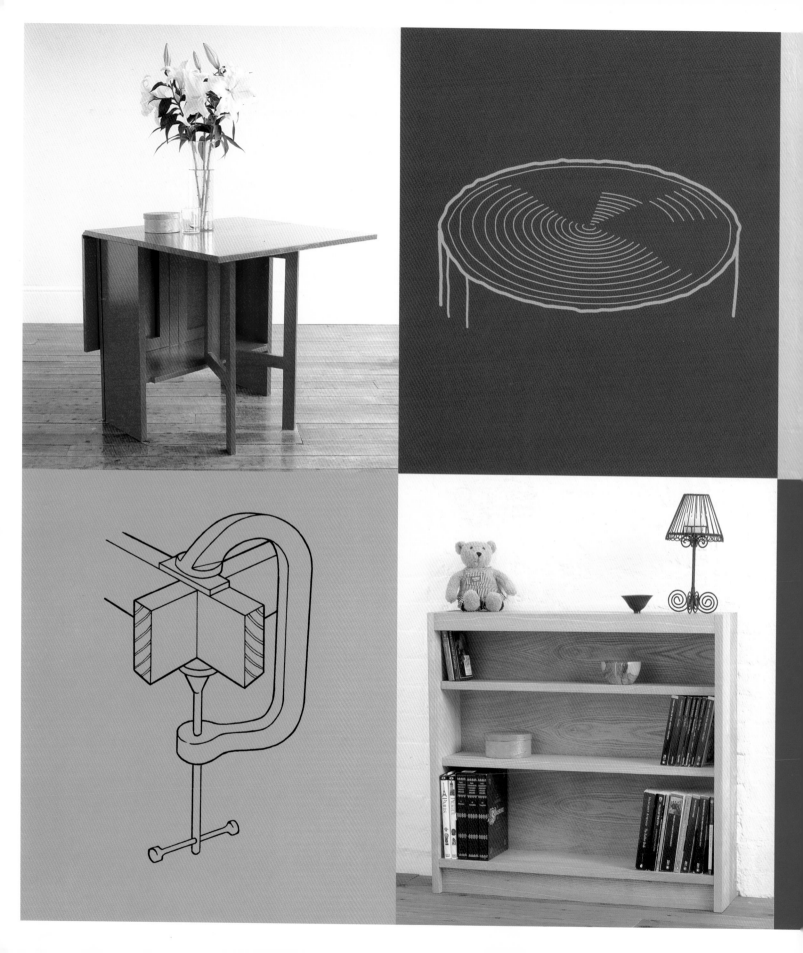

CHAPTER I

EQUIPMENT AND BASIC PREPARATION

The equipment shown will give you all you need to make the pieces, but it is not necessary to own all of them. Base any purchases on the specific needs of each project, and build your range of tools gradually. It is a good idea to start by mastering some of the basic techniques using scrap material.

EQUIPMENT

You do not need a wide range of tools or a sophisticated workshop in order to make the projects featured in this book. You can choose whether to use hand or power tools or a combination of both, but you will need a few basics. Each project is designed to let you use equipment that you already have or feel most comfortable using.

SURFACING TOOLS

For preparing a piece of wood to length, width and thickness you will use a hand-plane (jack or trying), an electric planer or a planer thicknesser (Fig. 1).

Hand-powered plane   *Electric planer*

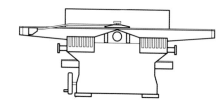

Planer thicknesser

Fig. 1 Planes

MARKING AND MEASURING TOOLS

For accurate marking out you will need accurate tools. These will include rules (tape, folding and steel), a try-square, a marking blade, a sliding bevel, a marking gauge (a mortise gauge), and of course pencils and pens (Fig. 2).

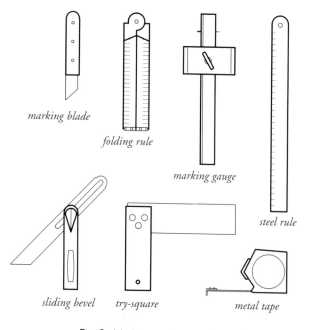

marking blade

folding rule

marking gauge

steel rule

sliding bevel   *try-square*   *metal tape*

Fig. 2 Marking and measuring tools

SAWS

You will need tools that cut both with and across the grain. For cutting timber to length (i.e. across the grain) you will require a crosscut saw, a jigsaw or a radial arm saw (Fig. 3). For cutting timber to width

Hand crosscut or panel saw

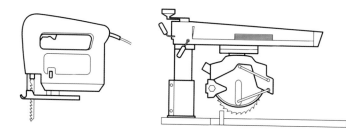

Hand-powered Jigsaw   **Fig. 3** Radial arm saw

(i.e. along the grain) a ripsaw, a circular saw or a saw bench (Fig. 4) will be necessary. If you do not have

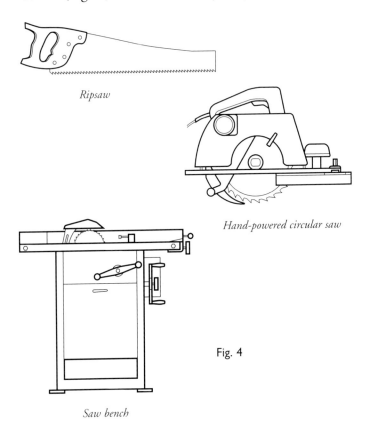

Ripsaw

Hand-powered circular saw

Fig. 4

Saw bench

both the crosscut and ripsaw, use a handsaw or panel saw with the teeth sharpened and set to enable rip cutting and crosscutting. For fine work you will need a tenon or dovetail saw (Fig. 5).

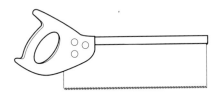

Fig. 5 Tenon or dovetail saw

Sometimes cutting curves will be necessary at the start of a project, but often this will be a process that occurs after the initial preparation has been finished. You will need one or more of the following: a coping saw, a keyhole (pad) saw, a bow saw, a jigsaw or a band saw (Fig. 6).

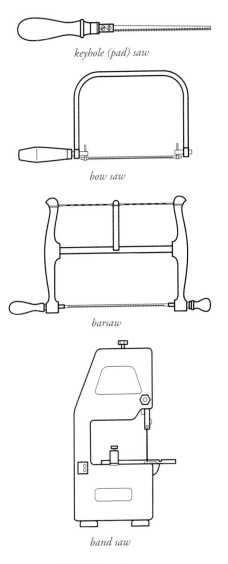

keyhole (pad) saw

bow saw

barsaw

band saw

Fig. 6 Saws for curves

The diagrams 7 to 11 indicate other important tools:

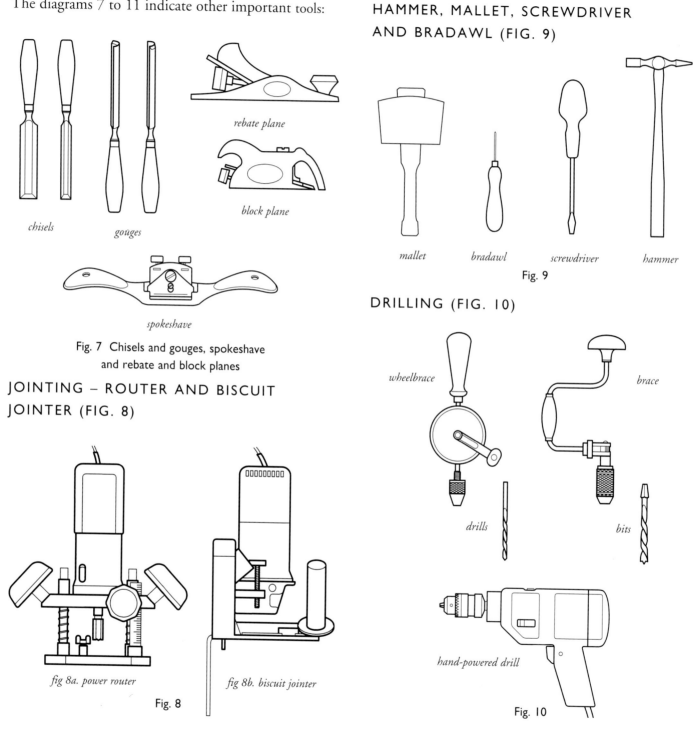

rebate plane

block plane

chisels

gouges

spokeshave

Fig. 7 Chisels and gouges, spokeshave and rebate and block planes

JOINTING – ROUTER AND BISCUIT JOINTER (FIG. 8)

fig 8a. power router

fig 8b. biscuit jointer

Fig. 8

HAMMER, MALLET, SCREWDRIVER AND BRADAWL (FIG. 9)

mallet

bradawl

screwdriver

hammer

Fig. 9

DRILLING (FIG. 10)

wheelbrace

brace

drills

bits

hand-powered drill

Fig. 10

SHARPENING (FIG. 11)

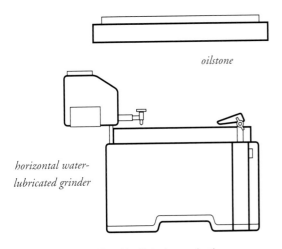

oilstone

horizontal water-lubricated grinder

Fig. 11 Grinder and oilstone

CRAMPS

When assembling a project you will require a selection of cramps. These could include sash cramps, G-cramps and/or web cramps (Fig. 12). Always try to assemble dry (i.e. without glue) before finally assembling with adhesive since you can more easily sort out any problems at this stage.

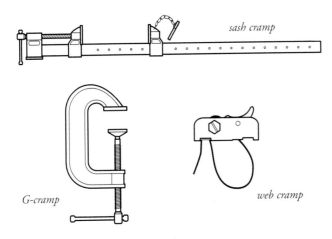

sash cramp

G-cramp

web cramp

Fig. 12 Cramps

FINISHING A PLANED SURFACE

For this you will need a scraper, scraper plane, abrasive paper and a sander (Fig. 13).

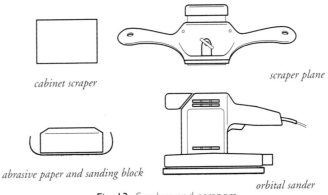

cabinet scraper

scraper plane

abrasive paper and sanding block

orbital sander

Fig. 13 Sanders and scrapers

For applying a suitable surface finish you will need brushes and mops, cloths and obviously a range of stains, polishes and waxes as appropriate. You will also need chisels for cutting or paring various faces and for cutting mortises.

Hand, power or machine planes can be used for surface preparation and finishing, and to further improve the surface you need either a hand scraper or a scraper plane. Abrasive papers in a series of grits from rough to smooth are also required. When making grooves, rebates and other sections, the router is a particularly useful tool. A large range of router cutters is available, enabling almost any section to be worked.

The other equipment required, such as drills, hammers, glues, nails and screws, is covered in greater detail within specific projects, but the information provided here should be a useful starting point.

BASIC PREPARATION

PROJECT ILLUSTRATIONS

For each project, clear step-by-step illustrations are provided to guide you through every stage of the making sequence. In addition, you will find plan drawings which tell you everything you need to know about the dimensions of each component and how they fit together.

When making any object, working drawings are essential. They are normally laid out as a series of views of the object to be made, generally as plans, elevations and sections. Each of these views relates one to the other and there are various conventions that dictate this relationship. The convention used here is third angle. Plans and elevations are fairly obvious, but sections are views, as if the object has been cut along a line that is defined on a drawing. Generally, it is a centre line but may be another 'cut' which must be specified on the drawing.

Even though all drawings are usually drawn to a scale, never rely on taking a measurement from a drawing with a ruler; always use the dimensions shown on the drawing. Generally the scales used are: imperial (feet and inches) 1 inch = 1 foot, or ½ full size (F.S.); 3 inches = 1 foot or ¼ F.S.; and sometimes full-size is used. Metric (metres and millimetres) 1mm = 10mm, or ⅒ F.S.; 1mm = 5mm, or ⅕ F.S.; and again full size. The drawings in this book are in proportion but not to scale.

Both imperial and metric measurements are shown throughout this book, but you will find that they do not tally exactly if conversion tables are used. Each system is worked out as a sensible set of measurements rather than arbitrarily converted from one to another.

Items are sometimes drawn in a way that represents how the item will look. In a technical drawing you may find isometric, oblique, or axonometric projections, but these never give a true visual representation of the item. In order to achieve this, it is necessary to draw in perspective, and even though there are perspective systems where measurements can be taken, most of the perspectives in this book will have been drawn freehand.

In working drawings, you will find different line thicknesses depending on whether the line is an outline, a sketch line or a dimension line and occasionally you will find dotted lines to represent detail and chain lines to represent sections etc. Often when a component is shown in section, that area may be hatched or shaded, both in working drawings and in the project illustrations shown in this book.

PREPARING TIMBER

The first job when using solid timber is to cut your sawn hardwood plank or sawn softwood sections to approximate length, width and thickness (Fig. 1). If you do not have a wide range of tools, your supplier may be able to undertake some of this work for you. Hardwood generally comes in plank form, while softwood tends to be sawn to standard sections. When you have brought your material into the workshop, it needs to be sawn into planks of the correct section, probably rectangular or square. Bear in mind that each component needs to be slightly longer than shown in the materials list. The sawn surfaces then need to be planed smooth, by surfacing with a plane or mechanical planer.

Start with the face side (a), ensuring that this is planed perfectly flat across its length and width, and that there is no bending, winding or twisting. Next, plane the face edge exactly square and straight with your first planed face (b). Check that both the face side and the face edge are straight and square, and when you are satisfied that they are correct, mark the wood to identify them (c). You can then gauge or mark the plank so that you can plane the board to its width (d) and then mark again so the board can be planed to thickness (e). If you are using a combination of a surface planer, a ripsaw and a thicknesser/planer it is only necessary to set fences and tables to ensure a precise result. With a hand plane (jack or trying) or an electric planer, this process takes a little longer.

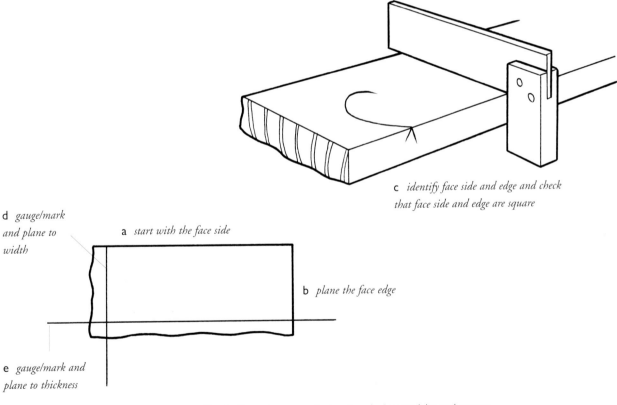

c *identify face side and edge and check that face side and edge are square*

d *gauge/mark and plane to width*

a *start with the face side*

b *plane the face edge*

e *gauge/mark and plane to thickness*

Fig. 1 Preparing sawn timber by planing straight and square

MARKING OUT

Precise marking out is absolutely essential. Cabinet makers usually mark with both knife and pencil (Fig. 2). Knife marks indicate where the wood is to be cut, while pencil marks show location of parts. You need a rule or straight edge to check that the timber is flat and not in wind, a square for marking right angles and a marking gauge for marking parallel with sides and edges (Fig. 3). If you are making a lot of mitres, a 45-degree square is also useful. You can use hand tools to mark a mortise and tenon (Fig. 4 and 5) or, if you prefer to work with hand-power or machine tools, you can use stops or jigs to achieve your desired result. It is always best to mark out in pencil before cutting joints, even with machinery.

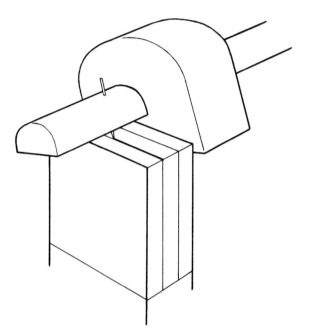

Fig. 3 Marking gauge to make lines parallel with sides and edges

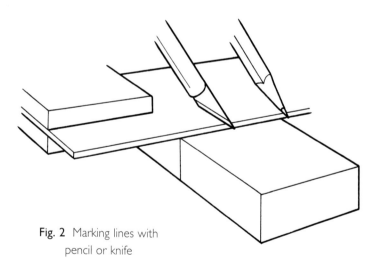

Fig. 2 Marking lines with pencil or knife

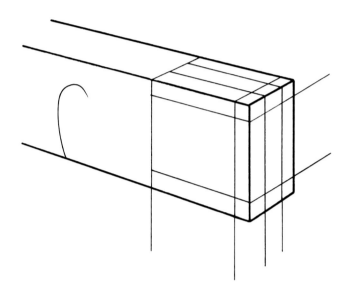

Fig. 4 Marking out a tenon

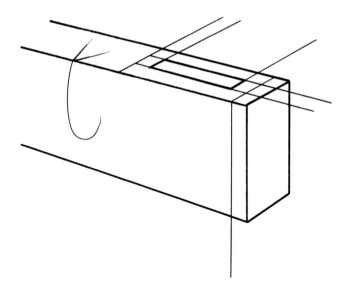

Fig. 5 Marking out a mortise

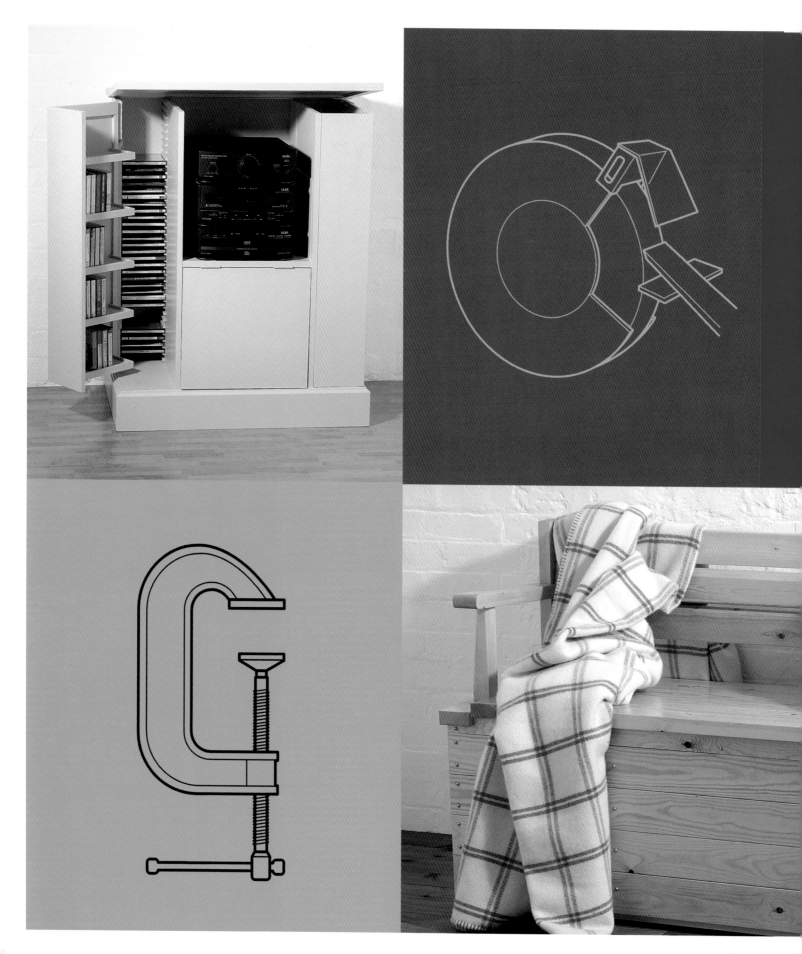

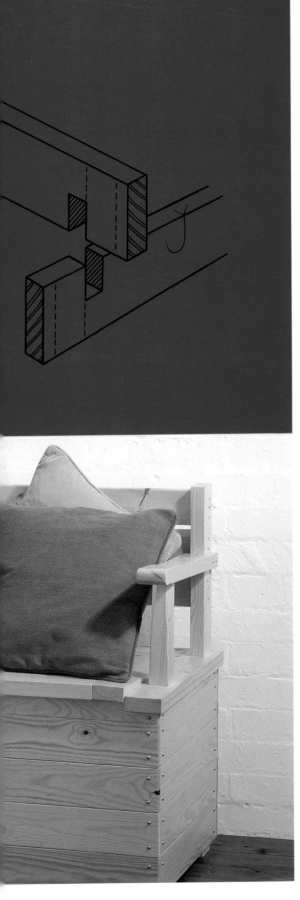

CHAPTER 2

THE PROJECTS

The projects which follow are suitable for woodworkers who are just starting out, as well as those with more experience. Whatever your own level of technical expertise, they are designed to enable you to enjoy the process of making the pieces while also developing your skills. Each project is supported by specific tips, as well as more general technical woodworking advice, such as working with timber, sharpening edge tools, using abrasives or finishing.

MIRROR/PICTURE FRAME

The frame is made from hardwood with a clear natural finish that gives it a country look. Its main feature is the unusual outward bevel, which gives a focus to the mirror or picture, and adds interest to a fairly simple piece. By changing the dimensions of the frame you will easily be able to make it a size to suit your choice of picture or mirror. Your selection of timber, its colour, grain pattern etc., will be determined by the background on which you wish to hang it. The method of fixing the ply back in place by means of screwed slips will enable you to change your picture easily or replace a damaged mirror.

MAKING SEQUENCE

1. Solid timber is required for this project (see the difference between solid wood and manufactured board on page 72). Your first task is to select a suitable hardwood (see softwoods and hardwoods on page 41). Then you need to prepare the components by cutting them to size and planing them smooth (see page 14).

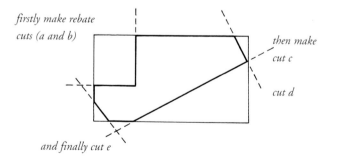

firstly make rebate cuts (a and b)

then make cut c

cut d

and finally cut e

Fig. 1 Making the beaded and rebated glass

2. The frame will have a mitre at each of the four corners. Before cutting them make the rebate (rabbet) to hold the glass (Fig. 1a–b) with a rebate plane, circular saw or table saw, and then make the bevels in the sequence shown (Fig 1c, d, e) with a plane.

3. Each of the pieces should be slightly over length to allow you to cut the mitres. These can be cut with a radial arm saw (Fig. 2a) or, very carefully, with a panel or tenon saw (Fig. 2b). You may need to plane the faces after cutting to achieve an exact fit.

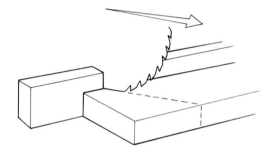

Fig. 2a Cutting a mitre with a radial arm saw

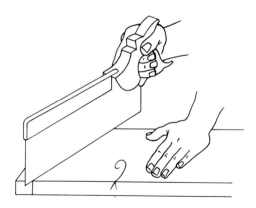

Fig. 2b Cutting a mitre by hand

4. Decide which type of joint you want to use between the mitre faces. If you use loose tongues, which are small pieces of plywood, the groove is normally made with a router (Figs 3a and b).

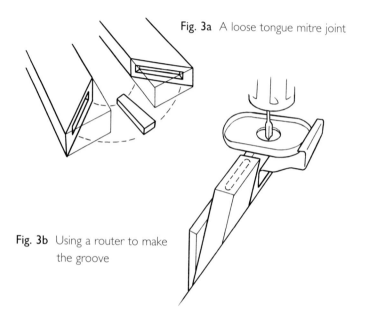

Fig. 3a A loose tongue mitre joint

Fig. 3b Using a router to make the groove

An easy and increasingly popular way to make joints is to use a machine which makes slots for keys – called biscuits because of their shape – on each face of the

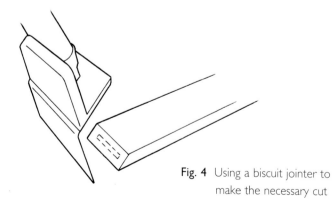

Fig. 4 Using a biscuit jointer to make the necessary cut

joint. If you have neither a router nor a biscuit cutter (Fig. 4), you can use dowels (Fig. 5), which need careful marking and drilling. Use gauges and knife lines to achieve a precise result if you choose this jointing method.

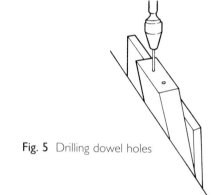

Fig. 5 Drilling dowel holes

5. After cutting the mitres, assemble the frame dry to check the fit and make any necessary adjustments. Ensure you have all the necessary tools to hand as you will need to work quickly and methodically during the final assembly. Use four cramps, two positioned underneath the frame in one direction and two above it in the opposite direction (Fig. 6a). Sash cramps are suitable for frames. Remember to put a piece of scrap

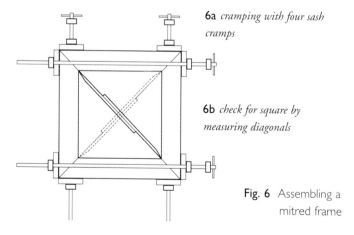

6a *cramping with four sash cramps*

6b *check for square by measuring diagonals*

Fig. 6 Assembling a mitred frame

wood between the jaws of the cramp and the work itself to avoid damaging the surface. Tighten up the cramps, close the joints and then check the frame for square by using either a square in the corners or, more accurately, by measuring the diagonals (Fig. 6b). If the frame is a little out of square, adjust the position of the cramps slightly. After checking that the joints fit precisely and that the frame is square, apply glue to all the surfaces that will meet and reassemble it.

6. Excess glue can be removed when it has cured to a rubber-like consistency while the frame is still in the cramp. It should peel off easily with a chisel. Do not wait until the glue has hardened completely because this increases the likelihood of damaging the finished surface. When the glue has dried, remove the cramps. Now you can complete smoothing the wood with sandpaper and apply a finish to protect and enhance the wood.

7. Make the back by cutting a piece of plywood to fit snugly, but not too tightly, in the rear rebate. Then make the four rebate slips that hold the glass, the picture and the back in place (Fig. 7). Drill two holes in each slip with clearance for the screw's shank and countersink so that the head will rest flush. Then put the glass and picture (or mirror) in place and insert the back. The four slips can now be put in position. Mark each slip for the side where it will fit and indicate the positions for the screws with an awl. Remove the glass, picture and back, and drill pilot holes for the screws with a small drill.

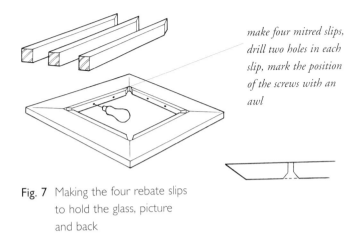

make four mitred slips, drill two holes in each slip, mark the position of the screws with an awl

Fig. 7 Making the four rebate slips to hold the glass, picture and back

8. Drill a small hole in the centre top of the frame at the back. This should be at a slight angle so the mirror or picture can be mounted on a vertical surface (Fig. 8).

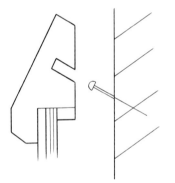

Fig. 8 Mounting the finished frame on a wall

Then sandpaper the frame and apply a finish. When this is dry, replace the glass, picture and back and screw the retaining slips in place. It is a good idea to use a touch of petroleum jelly or candle wax when inserting screws. This makes them easier to remove later. Certain timbers such as oak, for example, cause steel to corrode, and in this case brass screws must be used. If you use brass, always insert a steel screw of the same size first so that it cuts a thread in the wood, since a brass screw can easily break while being inserted. Then remove it and insert the brass screw. Finally, take a screw that fits the hole, insert it in the wall at a slight angle and hang the picture or mirror.

TIP
FRAME CONSTRUCTION AND JOINTING

Frames are fundamental to furniture-making, and the basic system of construction can be adapted to make different types of frame as well as underframes and tables.

With frames and underframes, rails are the crosspieces and the stiles are the uprights or legs. It is possible to make cabinets using frame construction and page 61 shows you how to make a panelled door following this method. In this case, the inside of the frame is either grooved or rebated to accept a panel. If you use a groove, the panel must be inserted when the frame is glued. The advantage with a rebate is that the panel can be inserted and then later removed after the frame is assembled (Fig. 9). This technique is used in the mirror project and in some of the others.

The traditional framing joint is a mortise and tenon of which several variations are shown (Figs 10a–e). Other basic woodworking joints suitable for frames include loose tongues, keys or biscuits, and dowels. It is also possible to use screws (Figs 11a–d).

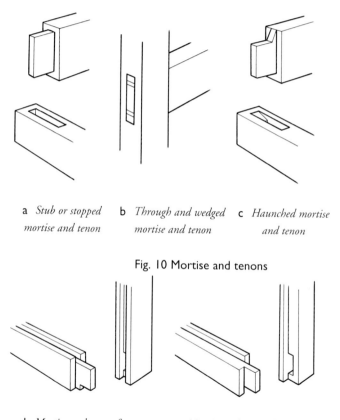

a *Stub or stopped mortise and tenon*   b *Through and wedged mortise and tenon*   c *Haunched mortise and tenon*

Fig. 10 Mortise and tenons

d *Mortise and tenon for a grooved frame*   e *Mortise and tenon for a rebated frame with long and short shoulders*

In this project, mitres are used as the best way of making the display frame. Your own choice of joints will depend upon your woodworking experience and the tools that are available to you, but you will see that even a novice maker can achieve good results.

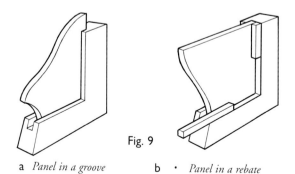

Fig. 9

a *Panel in a groove*   b • *Panel in a rebate*

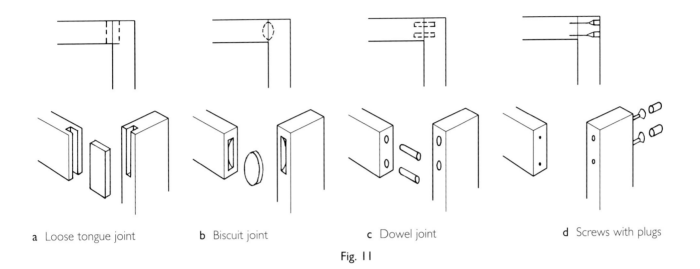

a Loose tongue joint   b Biscuit joint   c Dowel joint   d Screws with plugs

Fig. 11

MATERIALS LIST: MIRROR/PICTURE FRAME (NOMINAL SIZES: IN/MM)				
Item	*Quantity*	*Length*	*Width*	*Thickness*
Solid timber (for main frame)	4	16 in / 425 mm	2½ in / 60 mm	1⅝ in / 40 mm
Timber fillets (to hold ply/ glass in place)	4	12 in / 320 mm	½ in / 12 mm	¼ in / 6 mm
Ply back	1	11½ in / 315 mm	11½ in / 315 mm	¼ in / 6 mm
Glass mirror, or picture glass plus picture	1	11½ in / 315 mm	11½ in / 315 mm	¼ in / 6 mm
Screws	8	¾ in / 20 mm	no. 6	

CUSTOMIZING

MODERN

This version has a different section and uses paint or applied surface finish on one of the faces, i.e. textured paper or fabric. After assembling the frame, mask off the areas to be left with a natural timber look and apply the paint or wood dye, or stick down the applied surface.

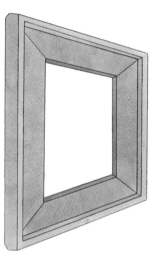

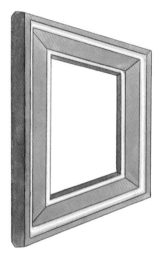

REPRODUCTION

This frame has a similar section to the modern frame, but it requires some extra shaping. A fairly dark timber, such as mahogany or walnut, should be used and the areas indicated in the illustration can be painted with gold or silver paint. Alternatively, they can be gilded if you are familiar with this technique.

DESIGNER

Similar in section to the country style, but it is possible to apply veneers to the front face. The example shown has a chevron pattern of dyed veneers but you can adapt this decoration using any type of veneer.

NB Measurements in solid wood are always slightly over in length, while width and thickness are finished sizes. However, when referring to suggested size in manufactured boards and glass, the finished size is given.

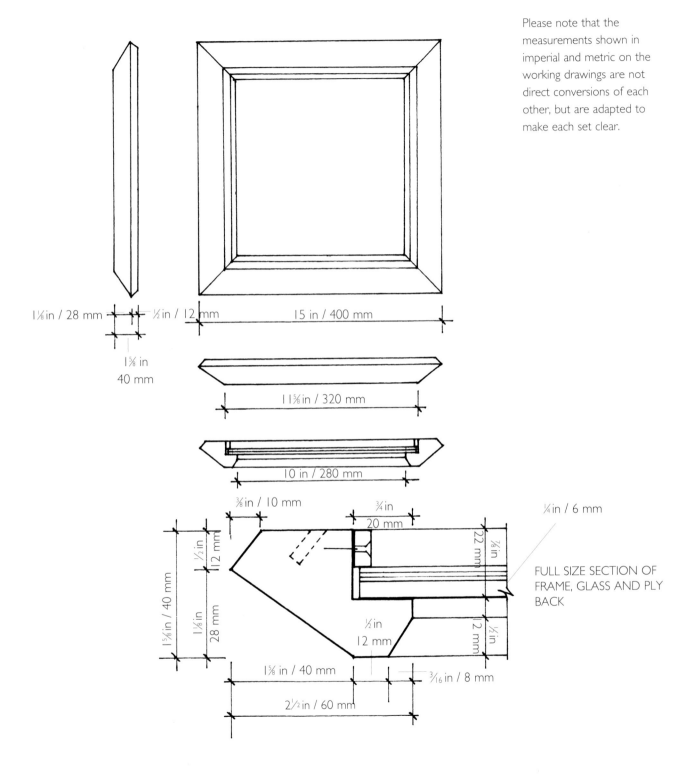

Please note that the measurements shown in imperial and metric on the working drawings are not direct conversions of each other, but are adapted to make each set clear.

1⅛ in / 28 mm   ½ in / 12 mm   15 in / 400 mm

1⅝ in
40 mm

11⅝ in / 320 mm

10 in / 280 mm

⅜ in / 10 mm   ¾ in
20 mm

¼ in / 6 mm

½ in
12 mm

22 mm   ⅞ in

1⅝ in / 40 mm   1⅛ in
28 mm

FULL SIZE SECTION OF FRAME, GLASS AND PLY BACK

½ in
12 mm

12 mm   ½ in

1⅝ in / 40 mm   ³⁄₁₆ in / 8 mm

2½ in / 60 mm

OCCASIONAL TABLE

This occasional table is an easy piece to make, the wooden framework adding interest underneath the glass top. The component pieces are simple – just four square legs, eight rectangular rails, a glass top and an optional glass shelf. This project gives experience in the basic preparation procedures, ensuring that timber is straight and square. The joints and assembly are very simple but give an interesting effect to the finished piece. Customizing options as shown allows you to choose your own changes. You will also discover how the table will look if you use different timbers to those shown in the photograph.

In the design shown, the top frame protrudes past the legs, but the bottom frame is flush with them, giving slightly more support to the table top. This also acts as a visual feature, but you could make both frames the same if you wish.

MAKING SEQUENCE

1. Prepare all the components by working the face sides and face edges, the width and the thickness (see page 15). When this process is complete, mark out the legs using a knife to show the length and a pencil on the two faces where the top and bottom frames intersect.

2. Mark out the rails in pencil, but use a marking knife and gauge to show the halving joints. Indicate the waste to be removed with pencil hatching.

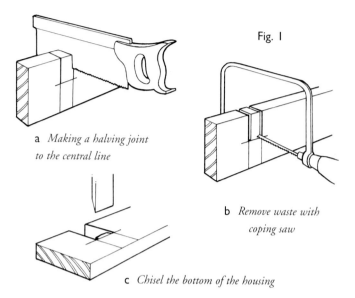

Fig. 1

a *Making a halving joint to the central line*

b *Remove waste with coping saw*

c *Chisel the bottom of the housing*

3. Cut all the legs and rails to length and then cut the halving joints. Saw to the central line and remove the waste with a coping saw. Use a chisel to trim the bottom of the housing (Figs 1a–c).

4. Before constructing the frames, mark where the frames will meet the legs and then mask all the areas to be glued with masking tape before applying a finish to the components. Scrape and sand the wooden surfaces to a fine finish and apply a coat of lacquer. If you prefer, sand the frames and legs smooth but wait until assembly is complete before applying the finish. Remove all masking tape, assemble the two frames, check that all the joints fit well and then glue up the frames. Halving joints are easy to fit – use a G-cramp to help close each one. Check the frames to see if they are square by measuring the diagonals and make any necessary adjustments (Figs 2–4).

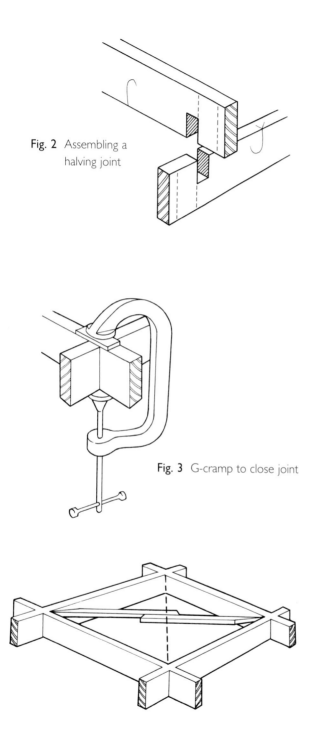

Fig. 2 Assembling a halving joint

Fig. 3 G-cramp to close joint

Fig. 4 Check for squareness by measuring diagonals

5. When the adhesive has cured, you can attach the frames to the legs. It is a good idea to use a screw as well as glue to fix these corners, although if you consider this unsightly, there is plenty of gluing surface to make the joint strong enough just using adhesive. To achieve a good bond, however, you need to cramp the joint firmly, so make some blocks from spare wood to fit into both the internal and external corners. Always remove excess glue when it is rubbery rather than leaving it to harden completely (Fig. 5).

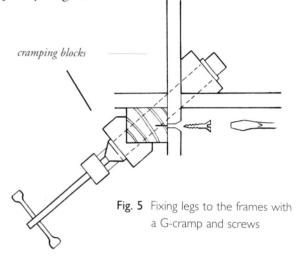

cramping blocks

Fig. 5 Fixing legs to the frames with a G-cramp and screws

6. Having glued all the joints, sand the table with very fine abrasive paper and then apply the final finishing coat (see Finishing, page 79). Complete the table by obtaining a glass top. You can use one sheet as shown or add a second smaller one if you wish to have a lower shelf as well. When using glass, it is advisable to have the edges smoothed or polished. The glass should also be toughened to make sure that it is no danger if it breaks. The glass should rest quite happily on the top of the table, but to prevent it slipping you could glue some small rubber bushes or discs to the

top of each leg. The friction will prevent the glass top from moving easily. The lower glass shelf will sit snugly in place, held in position by the legs.

SOLID TIMBER

Softwoods and Hardwoods

These terms are confusing as they do not refer to the hardness or softness of the wood, but to the botanical nature of the tree. Softwoods are coniferous evergreen trees with needle-like leaves. Their structure is composed of cells called tracheids, and food is transmitted from cell to cell through the side walls. Longitudinal pores, when present, are generally resin channels.

Hardwoods are deciduous trees which in temperate climates shed their leaves in the winter. The structure of the tree consists of long vessels or pores that transmit moisture and food vertically. In some species there are also horizontal 'rays' that distribute radially. Hardwoods from climates with defined seasons are normally 'ring porous' and show clear annual rings (Fig. 6), while those from climates with year-round growth are 'diffuse porous', showing less marked growth rings.

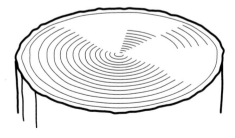

Conversion

Useful timber generally comes from the trunk of the tree, the branch wood normally being of little use because of the stresses present. The trunk is converted into planks by sawing. Due to the nature of timber, however, the resulting planks will move and distort, so it depends on the species and the timber end use as to how the conversion mill cuts the trunk. As the timber dries out, the annual rings tend to straighten (Fig. 7). Therefore it is better to saw the planks radially (quarter sawn – Fig. 8) rather than tangentially (through and through).

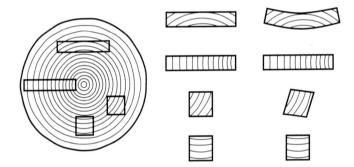

Fig. 7 As the timber dries, the annual rings straighten

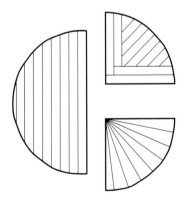

Fig. 8 Tangential and quarter-sawn planks

Seasoning

Before use, newly converted timber must have most of the moisture in the pores removed to make it stable. Therefore it must be seasoned, or dried. For exterior use, timber needs a moisture content of approximately 16 percent, for general interior work eight percent and in cases of high levels of air conditioning/heating even lower. The traditional method of seasoning is air drying. The cut log, which has spacers or sticks between the planks, is stacked in the open (but with a roof covering) to dry to the relative humidity of the air. Generally it is necessary to allow one year for every inch (25 mm) of thickness. When the moisture content must be reduced still further, or to accelerate the drying process, the timber is kiln dried. Kilns are basically large ovens with sensitive control of temperature and humidity, allowing the moisture content in the timber to be changed with precision.

ADHESIVES

There are many different adhesive systems now available for all types of materials. The ones that you will find most useful in woodwork are as follows:

PVA (poly-vinyl acetate)

A very good general-purpose adhesive that can be formulated to give high resistance to water. It is normally a white, creamy liquid which is directly applied to the faces to be joined. It sets or cures by the chemical reaction caused by the loss of moisture and this process can be accelerated in a heated environment.

Urea Formaldehyde

These are synthetic resin glues, which cure by chemical reaction. The commonest UF glue is available as a powder which, when mixed with water, forms a smooth liquid. It is important to mix thoroughly to eliminate lumps. When cured it is very water-resistant, but some formulations can be very brittle, making good tight joints essential.

Animal Glues

As the name implies, these types of adhesive are made from natural animal substances. Their main disadvantage is that they are not moisture-resistant. You may find natural glues still used for restoration purposes, but in general they have been superseded by synthetic glues.

Contact Glue

Normally rubber-based, contact glue is applied to both surfaces, and when tacky they are pressed together. It is fine for fixing rubber, leather and some fabrics, and is normally used when applying decorative plastic laminates in a non-industrial situation. However, do not use it for general woodworking or for applying veneer (see page 95).

Epoxy Glue

This is used mainly for fixing metals or certain plastics but not for wood.

Tape

Double-sided tape can be used in assembly operations, not as a permanent bond but for holding cramping blocks in place during assembly. Masking tape can be useful as an occasional 'third hand'.

Item	Quantity	Length	Width	Thickness
MATERIALS LIST: OCCASIONAL TABLE (NOMINAL SIZES: IN/MM)				
Legs (solid timber)	4	19 in / 470 mm	2 in / 50 mm	2 in / 50 mm
Rails (solid timber)	8	24 in / 600 mm	2½ in / 60 mm	¾ in / 20 mm
Glass for top (edges smoothed, sharp corners rounded)	1	24 in / 600 mm	24 in / 600 mm	⅜ in / 9 mm
Glass for lower shelf (edges smoothed, corners cut to 45° angle ½ in or 12 mm from each corner)	1	18 in / 450 mm	18 in / 450 mm	¼ in / 6 mm
Screws	8	1¾ in / 40 mm	no. 8	

CUSTOMIZING

MODERN

The construction is exactly the same but a coloured paint, wood dye or stain is applied. For the table top, use a sheet of frosted glass with a greenish-blue tinge.

REPRODUCTION

Here the main difference is that the table legs have been given tapered chamfers on the outside face. Use a relatively dark wood such as mahogany or apply a wood stain to give equally good results. A wooden shelf fitted into a groove in a box frame is substituted in place of the lower glass shelf. A simple mitred frame is used for the table top with a centre panel veneered with four separate squares of wood.

COUNTRY

The main difference with the country-style table, which could be made in pine, is that the legs are round in section. Construct a mitred frame for the table top in which a square of glass can be accommodated. The lower shelf is wooden rather than glass. Make a small quadrant cut in each of the four corners to fit the shelf in place. The lower frame can be secured to the legs with dowels or mortise and tenon joints.

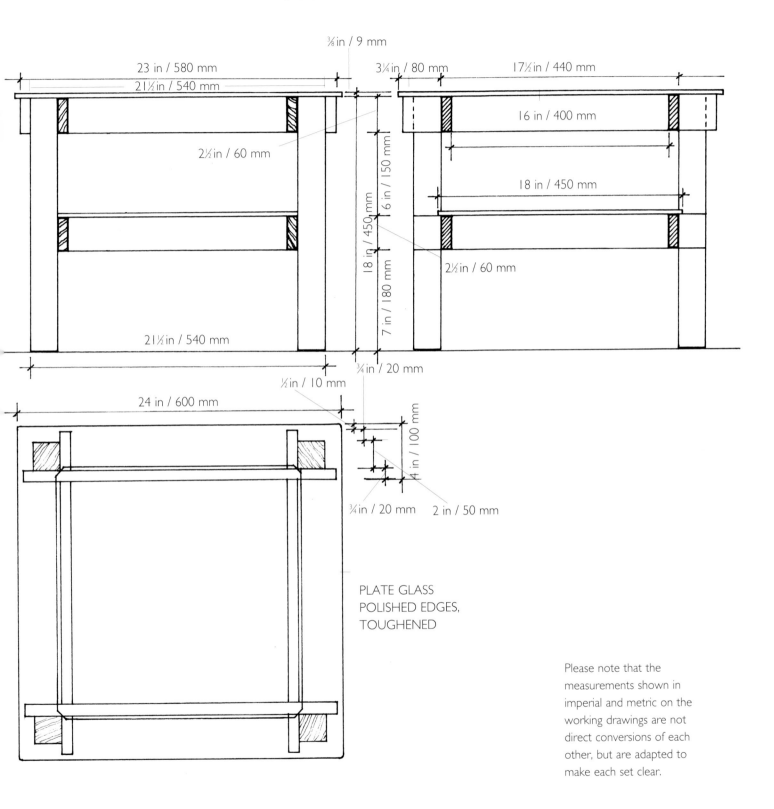

⅜ in / 9 mm

23 in / 580 mm

21½ in / 540 mm

3¼ in / 80 mm

17½ in / 440 mm

16 in / 400 mm

2½ in / 60 mm

6 in / 150 mm

18 in / 450 mm

18 in / 450 mm

2½ in / 60 mm

7 in / 180 mm

21½ in / 540 mm

¾ in / 20 mm

½ in / 10 mm

24 in / 600 mm

4 in / 100 mm

¾ in / 20 mm

2 in / 50 mm

PLATE GLASS
POLISHED EDGES,
TOUGHENED

Please note that the
measurements shown in
imperial and metric on the
working drawings are not
direct conversions of each
other, but are adapted to
make each set clear.

BOOKCASE

This bookcase is fairly low but the same design could be used at different heights. As long shelves will bow quite markedly under the weight of heavy books, the optimum length should be approximately 33 in (850 mm). Before you start, measure the largest and smallest book you are likely to want to store to determine the cabinet depth and the spacing between the shelves. Adjustable shelves are advisable in order to give more flexibility to your storage plan. The same principles apply when using the bookcase for objects other than books.

The project is fairly simple to make, especially if you have worked through the previous projects. It can be made from solid timber or manufactured board (see page.72). The illustration shows the project constructed in solid timber with a ply back and adjustable solid timber shelves.

MAKING SEQUENCE

1. Adapt the dimensions of the design to suit your purposes. If you have a lot of books it is best to make several bookcases rather than making fewer with longer shelves. If you are planning to make a single bookcase and wish to attach an external plinth and frieze, the finished piece will look more effective if you carry the frieze round the sides as well as on the front (Fig. 1a). However, with adjoining bookcases, the sides will need to be flush and the details confined to the front face (Fig. 1b).

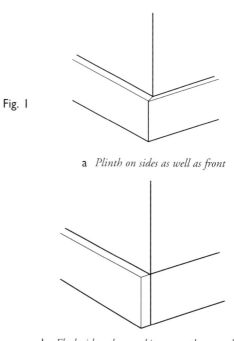

Fig. I

a *Plinth on sides as well as front*

b *Flush sides when making more than one bookcase*

2. Cut to length and width the two ends, the top, the bottom, the top front rail and the recessed bottom rail (Fig. 2), and work the grooves for the back in the sides and top.

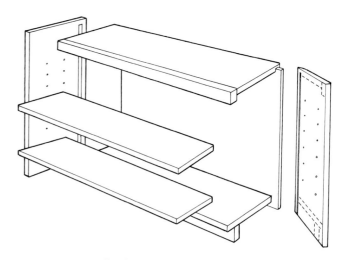

Fig. 2 Bookcase components

3. Decide upon the jointing system you wish to use (Figs 3a–d) and cut and fit the joints. All of these are options, but the choice will depend on your skill and whether you have a router or biscuit jointer. Dowels are the easiest. Test that the main cabinet will fit together properly by assembling dry without glue.

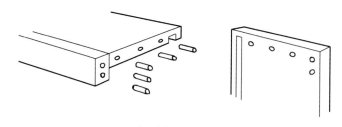

Fig. 3d Dowels

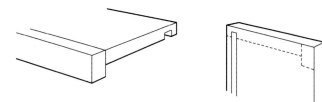

Fig. 3a Position of top and rail on the side

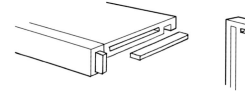

Fig. 3b Loose tongues in grooves on top and mortise and tenon on front rail

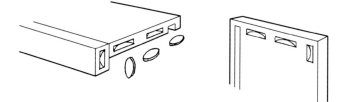

Fig. 3c Biscuit joints

4. Mark out and drill holes on the two sides to accept the shelf supports (Fig. 4).

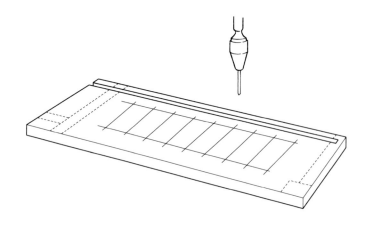

Fig. 4 Marked inside faces of the sides to be drilled for shelf supports

5. Then finish all the internal surfaces and glue and assemble the main carcass. When the glue has dried you can cut the back, fit in the groove and slip it in place from the bottom (Fig. 5), securing with screws into the rear edge of the bottom.

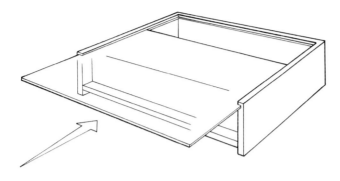

Fig. 5 Slide the back into the groove from the bottom

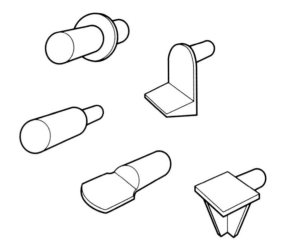

Fig. 6 These fittings simply fit into holes drilled into the surface

6. Mark, cut and fit the shelves and apply a finish both to the shelves and to the rest of the cabinet.

TIP

ADJUSTABLE SHELF SUPPORTS

The different types of adjustable shelf supports can be categorized into three main areas:

1. There is a wide range of fittings that slot into simple drilled holes in the side (Fig. 6). A simple way to make your own is to obtain some ³⁄₁₆ in (5 mm) brass rods, cut into sections in (25 mm) long and drill your holes to accept these at approximately ½ in (12 mm) depth. Another way is to use supports called magic wires. These are pieces of thin wire which fit into two holes as shown. The advantage here is that they are invisible since the wires run in grooves in the ends of the shelves. A similar system uses mini wires (Fig. 7).

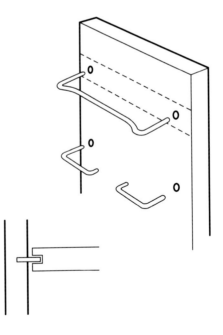

Fig. 7 Using magic wires and mini wires, the ends of which fit into drilled holes

2. Alternatively, you can obtain fittings of which the ends slot into sleeves that are set into holes. These holes are drilled and metal sleeves (usually brass) are inserted. These will then accept a wide range of different-shaped fittings (Fig. 8).

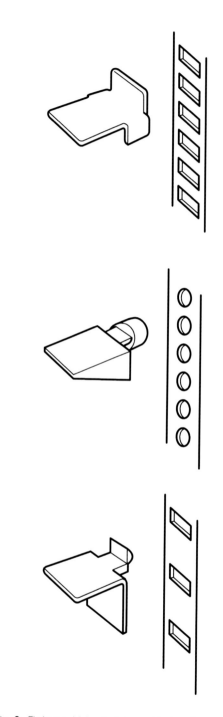

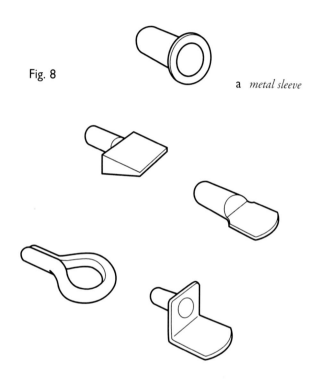

Fig. 8

a   *metal sleeve*

b   *Fittings which slot into sleeves*

3. Finally, you could opt for fittings which are based on pierced-metal strips which fit into grooves routed in the sides. These proprietary fittings require you to screw a metal strip into a routed groove. There are usually a series of perforations into which shelf clips fit (Fig. 9). When using glass shelves, select a fitting that will suit the design.

Fig. 9 Fittings which clip into vertical perforated strips slotted into the cabinet side

CHOOSING TIMBER

There are many different species of timber and your choice will depend particularly upon the colour, grain, pattern and texture that seem most appropriate for the item that you want to make. The following are just a few of the most commonly used timbers.

Softwoods

Softwoods are normally light in colour and there is a very wide range available. Though they are usually used in joinery and carpentry, they can sometimes be suitable for furniture.

Cedar *Thuja plicata* (yellow or Western red cedar) is even-textured and relatively stable. *Cedrus libani* (Cedar of Lebanon) is a different timber which is characterized by its aroma. It is often used for drawer bottoms to discourage moths.

Fir There are several different types of fir. Douglas or silver fir (*Pseudotsuga menziesii*) is mostly used for joinery. There are also many different pines including Parana pine, yellow pine, Scots pine and white pine, which are often used for joinery and furniture. Scandinavian or Russian redwood is a type of pine which is both attractive and fairly hard.

Spruce (*Picea* spp). This can be found in both northern Europe and in North America. Sitka spruce can be used for a range of items such as boats, gliders and musical instruments.

Hardwoods

Hardwoods can vary from almost white to virtually black. There is such a vast range of different species that only a few of the most commonly used are named here.

Oak (*Quercus* spp.). When freshly cut it is light. It is a high-quality furniture-making timber which stains and polishes very well.

Chestnut (*Castanea*). Similar to oak, this is a lightweight, pale wood generally used for turned items such as kitchen utensils and handles. It is also found in lightweight boxes and packing crates.

Walnut (*Juglans* spp). Found in temperate regions, this ranges from the dark brown of American walnut to the mid-brown European walnut. It is expensive and highly decorative and is therefore used for fine cabinet work and decorative panelling (in its veneer form).

Other useful types of hardwood are ash, beech, birch, sycamore and maple, which are all light in colour. Of the darker woods, the majority, including teak, mahogany, iroko and afromosia, are from tropical areas. Some fruit woods, particularly cherry, are also popular. There are some specialist timbers that range from very pale (holly and box) to very dark (rosewood, zebrano and ebony). Try to avoid purchasing timber that comes from a non-sustainable source. A great many species are now endangered through overcropping of forests, and timbers from managed plantations are becoming more difficult to find.

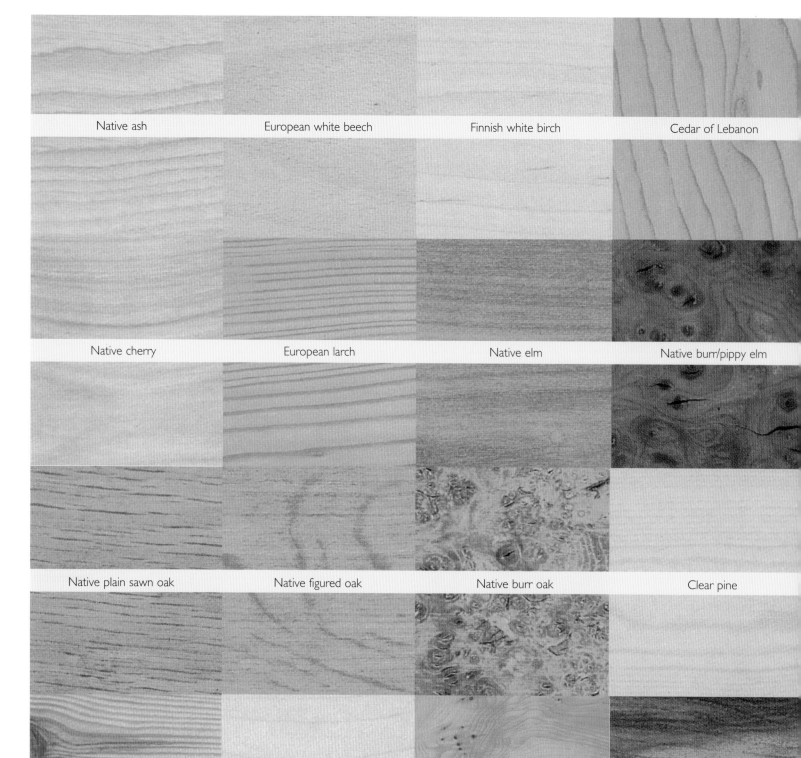

Native ash   European white beech   Finnish white birch   Cedar of Lebanon

Native cherry   European larch   Native elm   Native burr/pippy elm

Native plain sawn oak   Native figured oak   Native burr oak   Clear pine

Reclaimed North American pine   Native plain white sycamore   Native yewtree   Native walnut

SHARPENING EDGE TOOLS

The three main varieties of hand tools which need to be sharpened frequently are planes, chisels and gouges. Sharpening them ensures that they work effectively and avoids the accidents that can occur from the use of blunt tools.

The selection of planes ranges from those used for surfacing (trying plane, jack plane and smoothing plane), those used for detailed work (rebate plane and shoulder plane), short planes used for end grain (bull nose and block planes), those used to cut grooves, sections and mouldings (plough or moulding plane), a compass plane for rounded work and a small hand router to level off housings.

Chisels are all used for straight, flat cutting (firmer, bevel, paring and mortise chisels). Gouges can work convex or concave shapes and enable you to cut on the curve. There is also a wide selection of carving gouges. There are additional tools which will need their cutting edges sharpening. These include spokeshaves, scrapers, scraper plane and scratch stock (for working mouldings).

The sharpening process below is suitable for all of the above tools with the exception of the scraper plane and scratch stock (see Tip page 44).

First, grind the tool with either a high-speed grinding wheel (Fig. 10a) or a whetstone (Fig. 10b) at an angle of 25 degrees. When using a high-speed grinder cool

the blade in water, because if the blade becomes too hot the temper of the steel will be removed and a sharp edge will be difficult to achieve. Whetstones revolve more slowly and are water-lubricated.

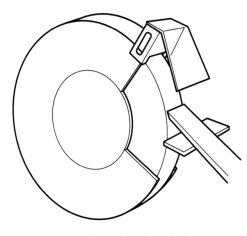

a *High-speed grinding wheel*

Fig. 10 Grinding

b *Grinding on a horizontal whetstone*

Once it has a straight and square ground angle, the tool should next be honed on a stone. The stones can be either natural or man-made and often use oil as a lubricating medium. They come in many grades from extra coarse to extra fine. For a beginner, it is best to use a carborundum stone with one face medium grade and another face fine grade. Lubricate the stone and work the blade up and down to create an edge, making the honing angle 30 degrees (Fig. 11a). Then turn the blade over and remove the burr (Fig. 11b). Continue the honing process, but work down from medium to fine grade until you have a sharp edge.

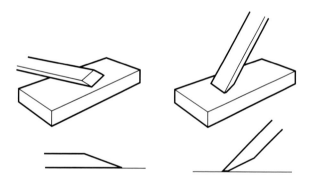

Fig. 11a Using the oilstone to work the honed bevel

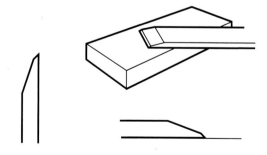

Fig. 11b Removing the burr from the back

After using the stone to do the honing, a leather strop can be used to achieve the best possible edge.

When sharpening gouges, you will have to use both the oilstone and the slipstone (Fig. 12).

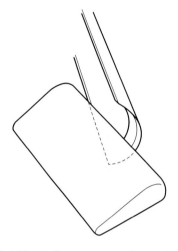

Fig. 12 Using a slipstone when sharpening a gouge

TIP
SCRAPERS
When sharpening a scraper you will initially need to ensure that the edge is straight. Next, make a burr from the faces and then turn the burr (see page 45 Fig. 13a) using a burnisher or ticketer. The scraper plane is easier to use and to sharpen if you are not expert with woodworking tools (Fig. 13b). When making a shaped cutter for the scratch stock, simply grind the shape on the cutter (normally a piece of broken hacksaw blade). It will be sharp enough to make the moulding shape that you require. A scratch stock is often made rather than purchased (Fig. 13c).

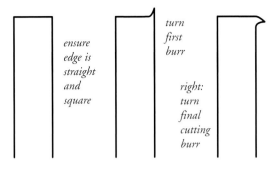

a *Making and turning the burr*

Fig. 13

b *Scraper plane*

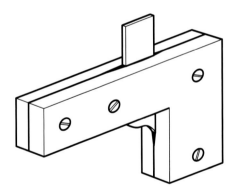

c *Scratch stock*

ABRASIVES

A timber surface must be prepared thoroughly before using abrasive papers, since it is difficult to remove surface blemishes with abrasive paper alone. Ensure that the surface is planed as finely as possible and if you have problems with the grain, use a scraper or a scraper plane. When using abrasive paper, use the full range of grades from rough to very smooth, since any scratches coming from the paper will be removed by the next finest grade. It is essential to keep the surface flat. Machines often have pads to keep the pressure flat and even, but when hand sanding use a timber or a cork block.

Hand-power tools include the belt sander, which can be used to remove a significant amount of timber, but you need a light touch and care must be taken with corners and edges as it is easy to sand off too much. A disc sander used as an 'add-on' to an electric drill is only suited to the fast removal of timber on shaped surfaces. When mounted on a small machine it is excellent for sanding endgrain, but again, you have to be careful not to take off too much wood. The orbital or reciprocating sander is useful once the preparation work has been done. Use the full range of grades of paper as above.

Of the abrasive papers (or sandpaper), garnet paper is normally used for furniture-making and is available from grades 50 (very coarse) to 600 (very fine). When finishing and cutting back lacquered surfaces, a silicon carbide paper gives excellent results, particularly on synthetic resin lacquers, and allows you to achieve a really professional finish. Fine wire wool is used for a final finishing after the finest grade of paper.

CUSTOMIZING

The design as shown is a simple modern bookcase but made to a low height of 31 in (800 mm). These customization drawings show that it is also possible to make the same design to a height to fit in with your own requirements.

COUNTRY

This uses a similar method of construction but an extra stile is attached to the front of the bookcase so that the vertical element is emphasized and the wood grain is shown off better. In addition, a small plinth has been added as a feature.

REPRODUCTION

This uses the same standard construction as the modern version but shows how you can add features so that it will fit in with more traditional furniture. Details that can be changed include the top cornice and the plinth. These details can be included on the sides if you make a single unit, so that your new unit can match with your existing furniture. If you do not have any furniture you wish to copy, look at the details in the corner cupboard (see page 92) which could be adapted for this piece. On the plinth the top surface could be bevelled, or a moulding could be added. This version shows two glazed doors which are hinged onto the front of the cabinet sides.

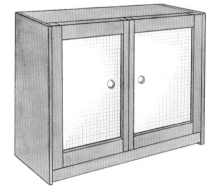

DESIGNER

This version is similar to the basic modern piece but here the bottom front shelf and the top are set back so that the doors fit within the edge of the sides. This piece could be glazed, but interesting effects could be achieved by using wired glass or expanded metal mesh.

Item	Quantity	Length	Width	Thickness
Sides (manufactured board)	2	32 in / 810 mm	10 in / 250 mm	¾ in / 18 mm
Top (manufactured board)	1	35 in / 900 mm	9 in / 225 mm	¾ in / 18 mm
Bottom (manufactured board)	1	35 in / 900 mm	9¼ in / 230 mm	¾ in / 18 mm
Top rail (solid timber)	1	35 in / 900 mm	2 in / 50 mm	1 in / 25 mm
Bottom 'kicker' rail (solid or board)	1	35 in / 900 mm	3¼ in / 82 mm	¾ in / 18 mm
Back (ply sheet)	1	34 in / 875 mm	29 in / 740 mm	¼ in / 6 mm
Shelves (manufactured board)	2	33½ in / 855 mm	8½ in / 215 mm	¾ in / 18 mm
Shelving pegs & holes (for plain holes or brass sleeves)	8 pegs and/or 32 sleeves			

MATERIALS LIST: BOOKCASE (NOMINAL SIZES: IN/MM)

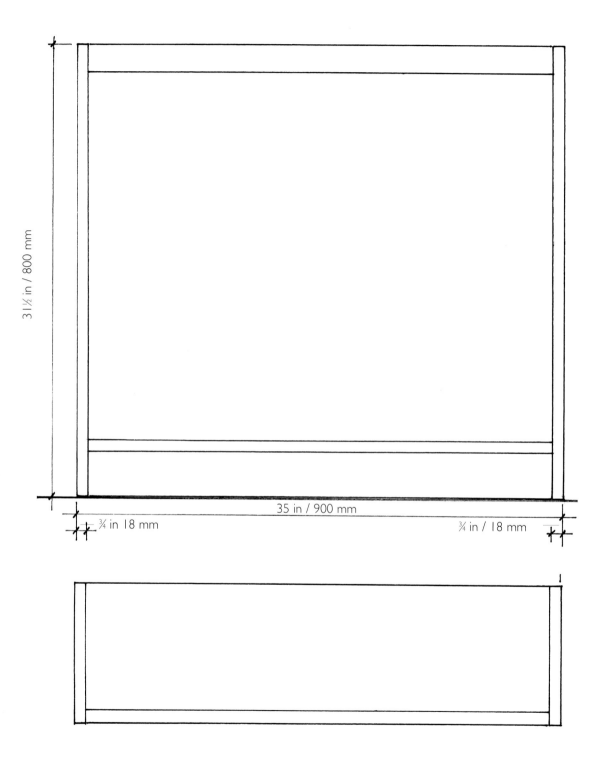

31½ in / 800 mm

35 in / 900 mm

¾ in 18 mm

¾ in / 18 mm

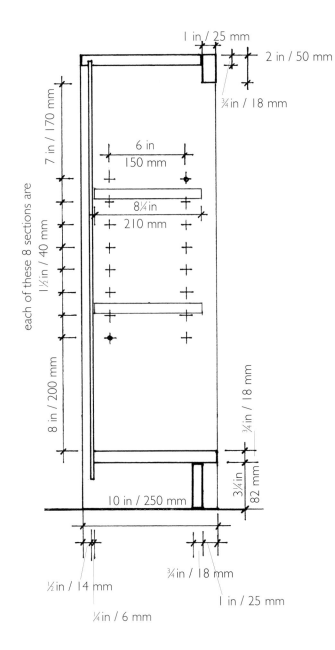

1 in / 25 mm

2 in / 50 mm

¾ in / 18 mm

7 in / 170 mm

6 in
150 mm

8¼ in
210 mm

each of these 8 sections are
1½ in / 40 mm

8 in / 200 mm

¾ in / 18 mm

10 in / 250 mm

3¼ in
82 mm

½ in / 14 mm

¾ in / 18 mm

1 in / 25 mm

¼ in / 6 mm

Please note that the measurements shown in imperial and metric on the working drawings are not direct conversions of each other, but are adapted to make each set clear.

MAGAZINE RACK

This is a very simple piece to make but it does require some precise marking, as well as careful grooving and cutting. The three style options given can be varied to your taste by the introduction of colour, stains, pattern, texture and shape.

MAKING SEQUENCE

1. To make the base, saw and plane the timber to a rectangular block and mark out the angles and grooves (Fig. 1).

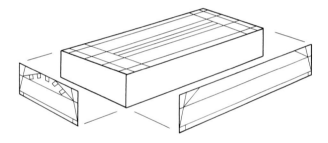

Fig. 1 The rectangular block marked out with angles and grooves

2. Before finally shaping, cut the five grooves. One way that this can be done is with a saw, preferably a circular or table saw. The blade can be angled to the table or the saw base, so it is easiest to leave the base square and make the grooves by taking a series of five cuts in the sequence – in the centre and in the two inside and two outside grooves (Fig. 2). This process can also be carried out with a router, but here it is not possible to angle or cant the cutter relative to the router base. Therefore make the centre cut, then make the angled faces so that you can rout the two grooves either side of

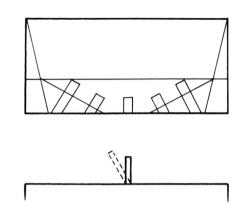

Fig. 2 Cutting the grooves with a table saw, passing the square block over the blade while working against a fence

the centre cut (Fig. 3). After you have made the grooves using either method, work the other angles as shown by the lighter lines.

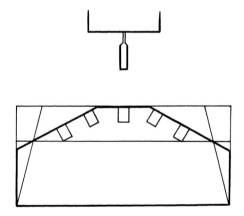

Fig. 3 Cutting the grooves with a router on the shaped block

3. To make the fins, mark and cut the five sheets to the required shapes, making the centre fin with ⅜ in (9 mm) ply and the other four with ¼ in (6 mm) ply (Fig. 4).

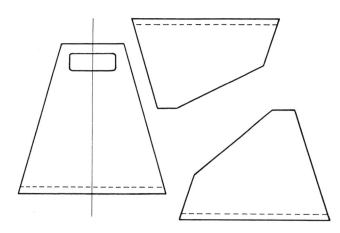

Fig. 4 The three shapes required for the five fins

4. Make the handhold in the centre fin. For this, use a coping saw or jigsaw to cut the hole and then chisel or file the edges and sand them. Apply two half round pieces with glue to give a more comfortable handhold (Fig. 5).

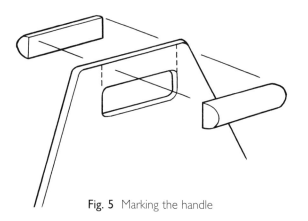

Fig. 5 Marking the handle

5. Fit all five fins into the grooves, then sandpaper all parts. Mark on the bottom of each fin the depth of the groove and mask both that area of the fins and the grooves with masking tape (Fig. 6).

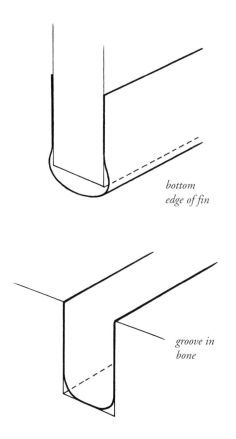

bottom edge of fin

groove in bone

Fig. 6 Covering the areas to be glued with masking tape prior to finishing the fins and base

6. Apply the finish before joining the components together. Once it has cured remove the masking tape and glue the fins in place. Starting with the centre one, remove the excess glue and let it harden. Then fit the two inside fins and again remove the excess and allow to harden. Finally, repeat with the two outside fins.

The piece illustrated in Fig. 6 has a small rebate on the bottom edge, but you could choose to add some simple feet to the underside (see Fig. 7).

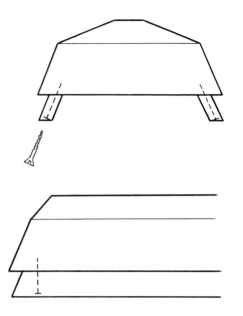

Fig. 7 Simple feet can be added

COLOUR, PATTERN AND TEXTURE

The range of natural timbers available offers an exciting selection of colours, patterns and textures (see choosing timber, page 41). The woodworker can choose to use the natural colour variations which are characteristic of different species, or stains to enhance or alter the colour. Grains of timbers can vary from subtle to quite pronounced patterns and textures. Decorative grain features are fiddlebacks, burrs and interlocking grains, which can be found on many exotic hardwoods. These can look effective when combined with a suitable project.

Timbers naturally have different textures, from a very fine surface with a close-grained material to much more open surfaces with timbers such as oak. A walnut gunstock can show a beautiful range of textures. Finishes also vary greatly from high gloss to a matt, open effect (see finishing, page 79). Timbers can be scrubbed, wire-brushed or sandblasted to give particular surface textures. Softwoods can even be burnt with a paint stripper to produce an interesting surface and colour. If you want a more marked texture, you can of course add this to a surface by light scratching or carving.

To alter the colour of timber, you can stain lighter woods with primary or other bright colours which can give unexpectedly effective results while still showing the natural grain of the timber. Alternatively an opaque finish, such as house paint, will hide the grain with subtle or vibrant colours. Other options might be to apply decorative plastic laminates, metal sheeting, glass or ceramic tiles to the surface. You can also decorate surfaces by using stencils, liming wax, flat painting or grained and marbled effects (see also veneers on page 95).

CUSTOMIZING

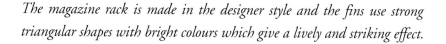

The magazine rack is made in the designer style and the fins use strong triangular shapes with bright colours which give a lively and striking effect.

REPRODUCTION

In this option the plywood fins are more traditional. It is a good idea for them to be faced with a dark timber such as mahogany or walnut and the ply edges stained to match. The handle is made as a round bar which is fitted to the central ply, giving a comfortable shape to hold. The base is shaped with a quadrant bead on the top edge and suitable reproduction-style feet are added at each corner.

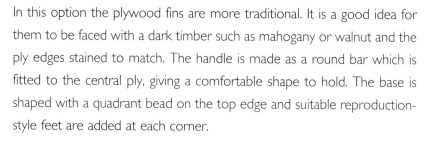

MODERN

This version has rectangular plywood fins with rounded top corners and the top handle is a round bar with its ends also rounded. The timber in this case should be light in colour, finished as natural wood, with minimal decoration to give a modern classic look.

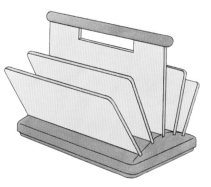

COUNTRY

Here pictures can be applied to the ply shapes. These can be cut out illustrations (decoupage) or you can draw out your own and paint them, choosing any theme that interests you. As long as you retain the hand-hold, the top of the ply fins can be shaped to suit the picture. If you do not wish to add pictures, the fins can be painted and patterns stencilled onto the faces.

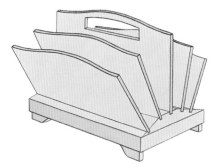

MATERIALS LIST: MAGAZINE RACK (NOMINAL SIZES: IN/MM)

Item	Quantity	Length	Width	Thickness
Base (solid timber)	1	18 in / 450 mm	4¾ in / 120 mm	2 in / 50 mm
Central support (ply, larger L & W to allow cutting to shape)	1	15 in / 375 mm	15 in / 375 mm	⅜ in / 9 mm
Side supports (ply, larger L & W to allow cutting to shape)	2	15 in / 375 mm	12 in / 300 mm	¼ in / 6 mm
Outside supports (ply, larger L & W to allow cutting to shape)	2	15 in / 375 mm	10 in / 250 mm	¼ in / 6 mm
Half round scrap solid timber to make handles comfortable	2	5 in / 130 mm	½ in / 12 mm radius	

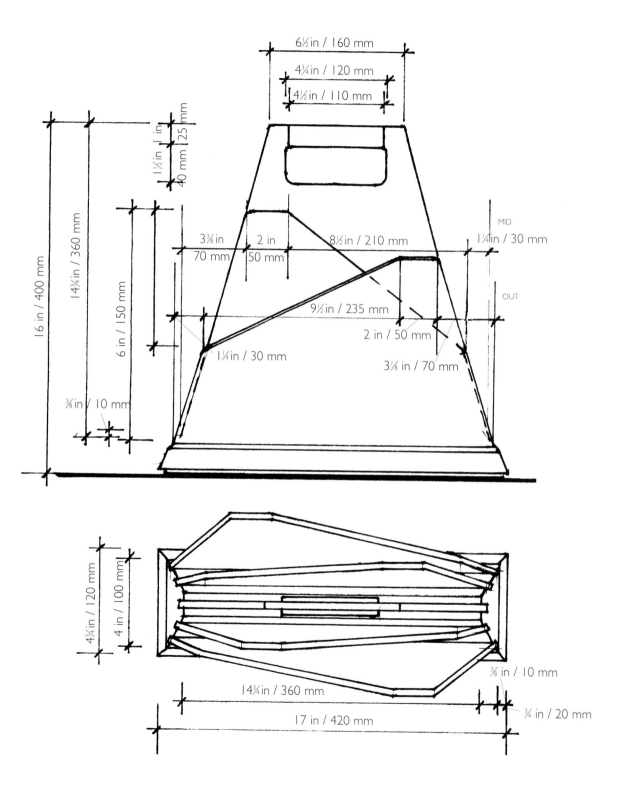

6½ in / 160 mm
4¾ in / 120 mm
4½ in / 110 mm

MID

1½ in / 1 in / 25 mm
40 mm

16 in / 400 mm
14¾ in / 360 mm
6 in / 150 mm

3⅜ in / 70 mm
2 in / 50 mm
8½ in / 210 mm
1¼ in / 30 mm

OUT

9½ in / 235 mm
2 in / 50 mm
1¼ in / 30 mm
3⅛ in / 70 mm

⅜ in / 10 mm

4¾ in / 120 mm
4 in / 100 mm

⅜ in / 10 mm
14¾ in / 360 mm
¾ in / 20 mm
17 in / 420 mm

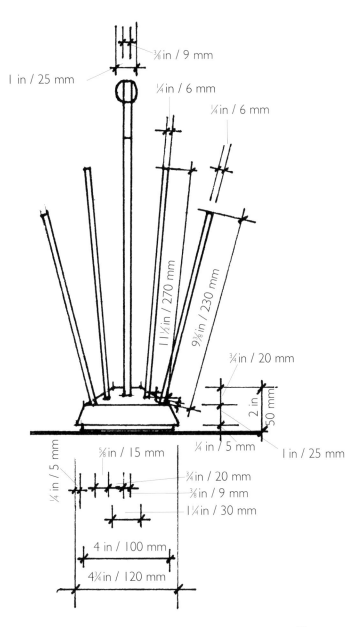

⅜ in / 9 mm

1 in / 25 mm

¼ in / 6 mm

¼ in / 6 mm

11½ in / 270 mm

9⅜ in / 230 mm

¾ in / 20 mm

2 in / 50 mm

¼ in / 5 mm

1 in / 25 mm

¼ in / 5 mm

⅝ in / 15 mm

¾ in / 20 mm

⅜ in / 9 mm

1¼ in / 30 mm

4 in / 100 mm

4¾ in / 120 mm

Please note that the measurements shown in imperial and metric on the working drawings are not direct conversions of each other, but are adapted to make each set clear.

WALL-HUNG CABINET

The size and design of the cabinet should be based on its intended purpose and the size of objects it will contain. The dimensions shown can be scaled to increase or reduce height, width or depth. When choosing solid wood, consider the range of colours available with reference to its environment and how easy the wood is to use. For the more experienced craftsman, the traditional jointing system can be used; the simpler methods described are suitable alternatives. First cut all the components to just oversize and then mark them out precisely. Then work either the groove or the rebate to fit the back.

MAKING SEQUENCE

1. You will need to joint the timber after purchase to give the required width. This can be an advantage, since a wide plank will be more liable to cupping than narrower planks which have been joined.

2. Start with the four corner joints of the carcass. The method of making mitres and holding them together with tongues, biscuits or dowels has already been outlined (see pages 20–2). Cut the mitres and ensure they are a good fit (Fig. 1).

3. If the jointing system has tongue and groove, the router is the ideal tool. Ensure the grooves are placed near the inside corner so that there is no danger of the tongues (or, if using a jointer, the biscuits) weakening the wood (Fig. 2).

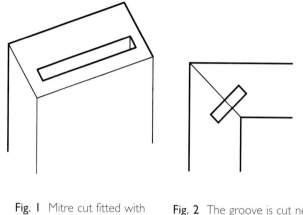

Fig. 1 Mitre cut fitted with groove in place

Fig. 2 The groove is cut near the inside corner

4. If using dowels, make sure that they are precisely marked. Insert a fine panel pin on one mitre face at the dowel centres and clip off the head. The mitres can be brought together so that the pin marks the centre of the dowel on the other mitre face. You then have a precise centre for all the dowels. The pin can then be pulled out. Another method for dowels is to drill the holes on one side of the mitre and then use dowel centre points to mark the centre of the holes on the other face. If fitted vertical or horizontal shelves are to be included, a similar process should be carried out at this stage so that they will fit accurately in position.

5. Assemble the carcass dry to check that the mitres cramp up tightly. If you use sash cramps, you will need eight (Fig. 3). Another method that gives pressure to the joint is to glue some scrap wood to the sides and use G-cramps to close the joint. These are planed off after the final assembly (Fig. 4).

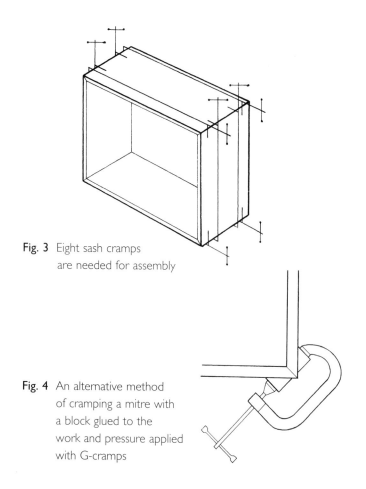

Fig. 3 Eight sash cramps
are needed for assembly

Fig. 4 An alternative method
of cramping a mitre with
a block glued to the
work and pressure applied
with G-cramps

6. It is preferable to have shelves that are adjustable and there are simple alternatives for this (see bookcase project, page 36). Vertical perforated strips with adjustable pegs is one option, or a series of small holes into which shelf supports can be inserted. Mark out and drill the holes for the shelf supports.

When making cabinets it is easier to finish the internal faces before assembly, so mark the joint faces and scrape, sand and apply your final finish to the inside. When this is dry, glue together and check that the cabinet is square.

7. Cut the back, checking that it fits in place. In the method used in (Fig. 5), the back slides in a groove which runs up two sides and across the top of the back of the cabinet. The rear edge of the bottom of the

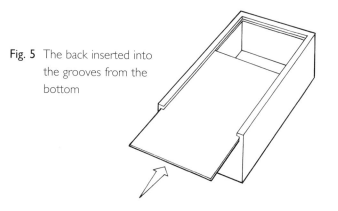

Fig. 5 The back inserted into
the grooves from the
bottom

cabinet should be in line with the middle face of the groove so the back will slot in from the bottom. The back can then be fixed along the bottom edge. An alternative method for fixing the back is to form a rebate and screw the back into the rebate (Fig. 6). Before fixing the back in position, sand and finish the carcass inside and out.

Fig. 6 The back dropped
into a rebate

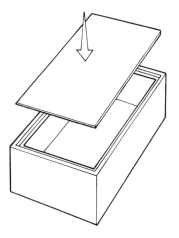

8. Make the door with two vertical stiles and two horizontal rails and mark out the mortise and tenons (Fig. 7). At this stage you should work the groove or

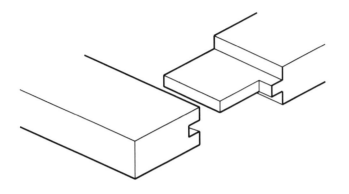

Fig. 7 Mortise and tenon

rebate that will accept the panel. Saw the tenons and chisel out the mortises. Fit them dry to ensure that the joints close properly. If the panel is to be solid timber or ply located in a groove, cut this to size. Sand and apply a finish. Whether you use grooves or rebates is dependent on your selection of panel material. If you choose ply or timber, use a groove; if you choose glass, use a rebate. Decide on the number and type of hinges required.

9. The door can now be assembled with glue (Fig. 8) and, when dry, fitted to the carcass by careful planing. Fit the hinges, swing the door and ensure it fits properly.

10. Remove the door and make and fit the shelves. Sand all the components and apply a final finish.

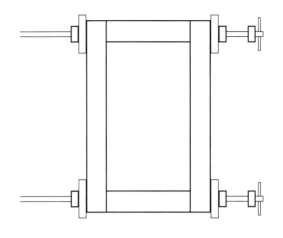

Fig. 8 Assembling the door

TIP

SOLID TIMBER CARCASS CONSTRUCTION

When making a cabinet you can choose from several different joints for the corners, including traditional ones that require woodworking expertise. When dovetailing wide boards it is necessary to have smaller pins at the edges, but wider ones can be used in the centre. For skilled craftsmen, a through dovetail enables the viewing of both the tails and the pins of the dovetail, which in itself forms an attractive decoration (Fig. 9).

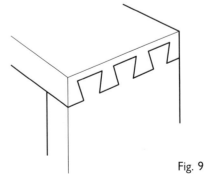

Fig. 9 Through dovetail

Other corner dovetails are lap dovetails (Fig. 10), double lap dovetails (Fig. 11) and secret mitre dovetails (Fig. 12). Simpler alternatives are cutting mitres, lap joints and double lap joints and using tongue and groove joints, biscuits or dowels to make the joint secure (see Fig. 13 & pages 20–2). If appropriate, screws can be used to reinforce these joints. Do not glue any form of corner without a fixing, as gluing timber on end grain does not create sufficient strength.

While solid wood can be used for backs, an allowance for timber movement is necessary, so it is advisable to use manufactured board. Even with good corner joints, a larger cabinet may rack and put pressure on the joints. The insertion of a back will stabilize the whole carcass. This is often aided by the insertion of fixed vertical or horizontal shelves and suitable joints for these are housings, or the simplest joints indicated in Fig. 13.

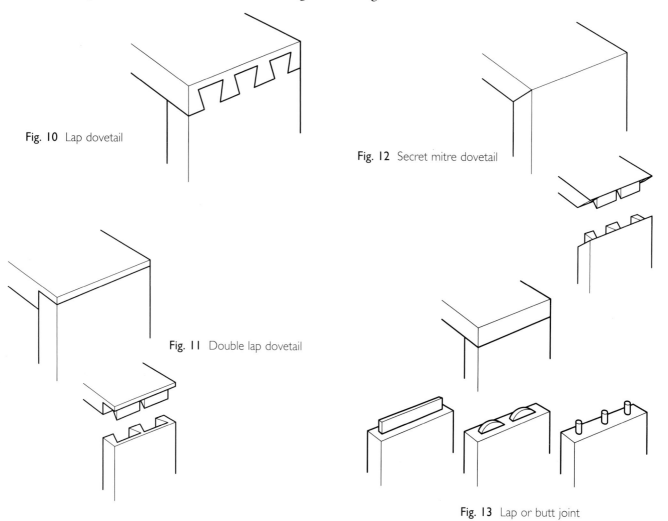

Fig. 10 Lap dovetail

Fig. 11 Double lap dovetail

Fig. 12 Secret mitre dovetail

Fig. 13 Lap or butt joint

TIP

FITTING BUTT HINGES

The type and positioning of a hinge and the critical hinge dimensions are shown in Fig. 14a–d and the following procedures will need to be worked on the cabinet side as well as the door edge as described.

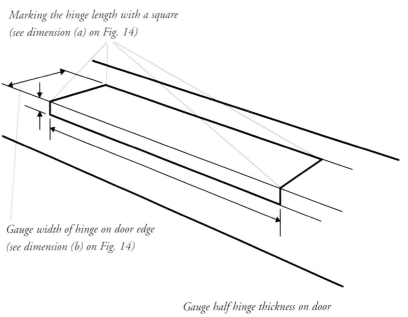

Marking the hinge length with a square (see dimension (a) on Fig. 14)

Gauge width of hinge on door edge (see dimension (b) on Fig. 14)

Gauge half hinge thickness on door face (see dimension (c) on Fig. 14)

Fig. 15

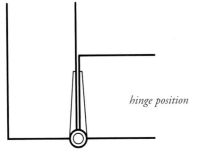

hinge position

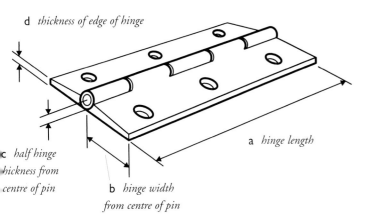

d *thickness of edge of hinge*

a *hinge length*

c *half hinge thickness from centre of pin*

b *hinge width from centre of pin*

Fig. 14 Fixing butt hinges – hinge dimensions and initial marking out

Mark the exact length of the hinge with a square on the edge and face of the door, preferably with a cut line (see Fig. 15 and Fig. 14a).

Gauge the width of the hinge on the edge of the door with a cut line marking from the centre of the pin to the edge of the hinge (see Fig. 15 and Fig. 14b).

Mark the hinge on the face of the door from the edge to the centre of the pivot or pin (see Fig. 15 and Fig. 14c).

Make some fine saw cuts at the ends, and at intervals, from gauge line to gauge line (Fig. 16 – insert shows saw cuts to lines (b) and (c) on Fig. 14).

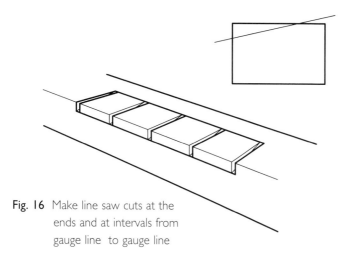

Fig. 16 Make line saw cuts at the ends and at intervals from gauge line to gauge line

Carefully pare out the waste with a chisel, noting that the edge of the hinge is thinner than its dimension at the pivot (Fig. 17 – insert shows dimensions (c) and (d) on Fig. 14).

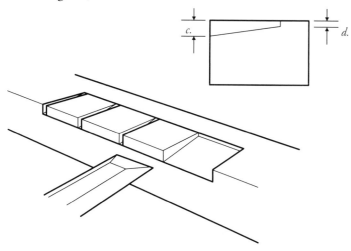

Fig. 17 Saw cuts are made at the ends and at intervals between, then wasted is pared with a chisel

Place the hinge in position, mark the centre of one hole with an awl, then drill a pilot hole and insert one of the screws (Fig. 18).

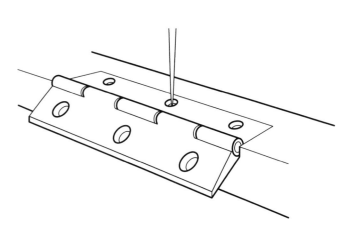

Fig. 18 Place hinge in position in the recess that has been cut as described and mark the centre of the hole

Offer-up the door to the cabinet and mark the position of the hinges on the cabinet side. Then repeat the above process.

When the door or flap is hung and swings and fits satisfactorily, fit the remaining screws.

CUSTOMIZING

The photograph of the piece shows the door as a frame with a painted plywood panel. Alternative treatments could have been to have the ply veneered with an interesting timber or to use a solid timber panel in the frame. The choice of timber will also greatly change the appearance.

MODERN

An alternative treatment is shown left. If the cabinet is to display items, obviously a glass door is necessary. You can use the door frame as shown in the main piece, in which case you will use a rebate instead of a groove and insert the glass in a similar way to that shown in the mirror frame (but obviously not with the plywood behind it). Such a cabinet can look very interesting if you have a sheet of glass with no frame but if you use this option you will need to buy special hinges and fittings and to ensure that the glass is toughened before final fitting to the cabinet.

DESIGNER

In this design a small roller blind is used. Such blinds are easily available and in a wide range of colours and patterns. A Venetian blind with very thin slats is also a nice idea. For a slightly larger cabinet you could use curtains or a Roman blind.

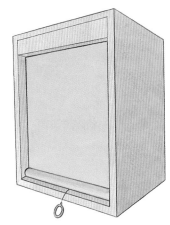

REPRODUCTION

It is a good idea to use a dark wood for this style. The cabinet could also be interesting with two doors instead of one, hinged on both sides and made of manufactured board with a figured or naturally patterned veneer. On something like this, use brass fittings. The illustration shows the application of a pediment detail. If you already have traditional furniture you could adopt a section from it as a pattern.

MATERIALS LIST: WALL-HUNG CABINET (NOMINAL SIZES: IN/MM)

The carcass is drawn 1 in thick – most solid timber is 1 in sawn and therefore finishes to approx. ⅞ in. Make the necessary allowance, or if using manufactured board use 13/16/21.

Item	Quantity	Length	Width	Thickness
Sides (solid timber)	2	25 in / 625 mm	9 in / 230 mm	1 in / 25 mm
Top (solid timber)	1	17 in / 425 mm	9 in / 230 mm	1 in / 25 mm
Bottom (solid timber)	1	17 in / 425 mm	8 in / 210 mm	1 in / 25 mm
Back (plywood sheet)	1	23¼ in / 580 mm	14½ in / 365	¼ in / 6 mm
Fixed hanging batten (solid timber)	1	14 in / 350 mm	1¼ in / 32 mm	¾ in / 14 mm
Wall fixed hanging batten (solid timber)	1	13 in / 330 mm	2 in / 50 mm	¾ in / 14 mm
Door stiles (solid timber)	2	23 in / 575 mm	2 in / 50 mm	¾ in / 18 mm
Top door rail (solid timber, length allows for mortise & tenon joints)	1	14 in / 350 mm	2 in / 50 mm	¾ in / 18 mm
Bottom rail (solid timber, length allows for mortise & tenon joints)	1	14 in / 350 mm	2½ in / 65 mm	¾ in / 18 mm
Door panel (plywood sheet)	1	18 in / 460 mm	10½ in / 270 mm	¼ in / 6 mm
Adjustable shelf (solid timber)	1	13⅞ in / 346 mm	7 in / 170 mm	¾ in / 18 mm
Shelving pegs & holes (for plain holes with brass shelves)	4 pegs and /or 24 sleeves			
Butt hinges	2	1½ in / 40 mm		
Catch & Knob	1 of each			

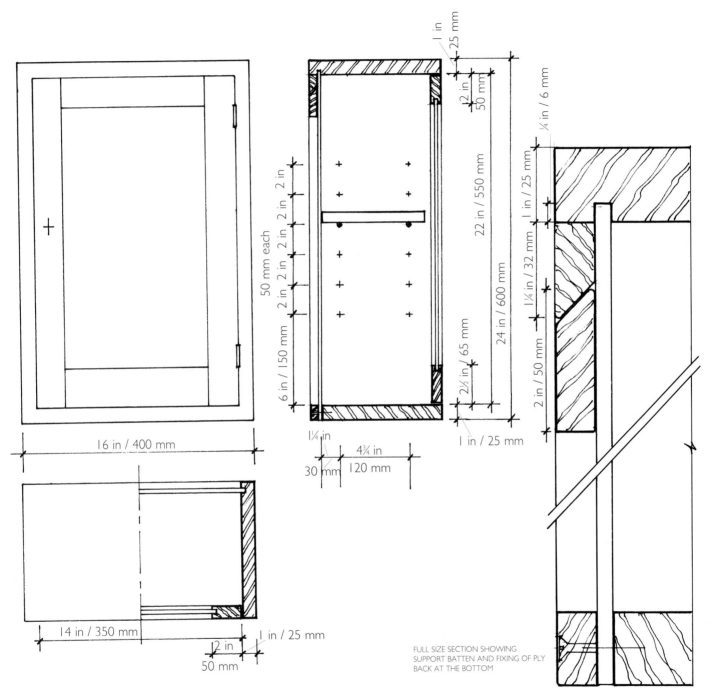

1 in / 25 mm

2 in / 50 mm

22 in / 550 mm

24 in / 600 mm

2½ in / 65 mm

¼ in / 6 mm

1 in / 25 mm

1¼ in / 32 mm

2 in / 50 mm

50 mm each

6 in / 150 mm

2 in 2 in 2 in 2 in 2 in 2 in

16 in / 400 mm

1¼ in
30 mm

4¾ in
120 mm

14 in / 350 mm

2 in
50 mm

1 in / 25 mm

FULL SIZE SECTION SHOWING
SUPPORT BATTEN AND FIXING OF PLY
BACK AT THE BOTTOM

Please note that the measurements shown in imperial and metric
on the working drawings are not direct conversions of each other,
but are adapted to make each set clear.

TV AND VIDEO UNIT

This project provides a functional, compact and appealing storage system for television and video. It has been designed with the average family portable in mind, but as in all the projects, the size of the unit can be adapted to suit your equipment.

The unit is designed for construction with manufactured board and you can then decide whether to have a painted finish or to use pre-veneered board which will show timber grain. The storage space shown here is designed to allow for the different-sized video covers which are available, and the method outlined below suggests including storage space on the shelves within the unit. If you would prefer to have drawers, see the Tips on pages 70–1.

MAKING SEQUENCE

1. Construct the basic unit, which consists of a top, bottom, back and central partition, using tongues and grooves, biscuits or dowels, depending on your toolkit (Fig. 1). As an alternative, it is also possible to screw

through the top and bottom into the back and centre partition, since the screws will not show.

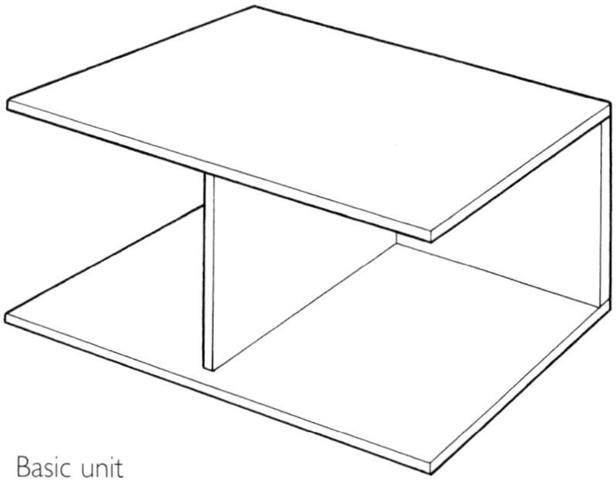

2. Add the plinth, which can be glued and screwed from underneath as shown (Fig. 2).

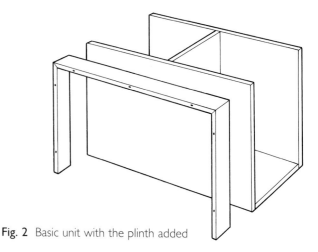

Fig. 2 Basic unit with the plinth added

3. The supports for the television should then be added (Fig. 3a). Before doing this check that the feet or support pads on the television will not sit directly on the video machine. If this does happen, you will need to add a shelf between the television and the video (Fig. 3b).

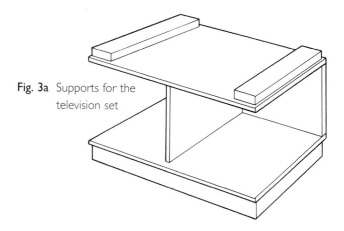

Fig. 3a Supports for the television set

Fig. 1 Basic unit

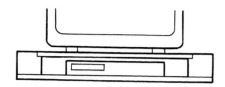

Fig. 3b A shelf could be added between the
television and the video

4. If you would like to store your videos by using the side-opening method, fit the centre front panel and the shelves in position (Fig. 4).

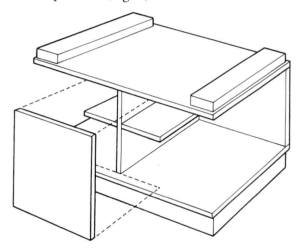

Fig. 4 Fitting the shelves and the centre front panel

5. Make the two side doors, remembering that one is right-handed and the other left-handed (Fig. 5). The shelves for video storage can be fitted in position, and they will reinforce and strengthen the L shape of these doors.

6. Hinge the doors in place and fit catches or locks (see page 113). After carrying out a dry assembly, you can remove the fittings, sand the piece and apply a finish.

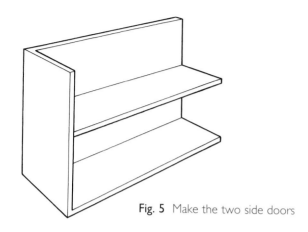

Fig. 5 Make the two side doors

TIP

DRAWERS

Follow these instructions if you would prefer to use drawers to replace the side-opening method above.

Firstly, fit the two sides in position (see Fig. 6a).

Fig. 6

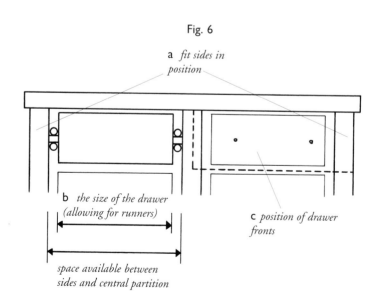

a *fit sides in position*

b *the size of the drawer (allowing for runners)*

c *position of drawer fronts*

space available between sides and central partition

Make sure that the drawer is the correct size to accept the video cassette cases. Use proprietary drawer runners that will allow the drawers to run fully outside the cabinet for maximum access. These should be available from your nearest furniture hardware merchants. Different makes will vary slightly, so check the amount of space that is needed between the sides of the cabinet and the outsides of the drawer and make the width of the drawer box to the correct dimensions (Fig. 6b).

The drawer itself is a five-sided box. The sides are thick enough to accept screws and the thin ply bottom is fixed with glue and screws or pins. This box can be made using simple lap joints on the corners, glued and screwed (Fig. 7), or can simply be butted together (Fig. 8), although some form of location would be preferable, i.e. screws or pins.

When the drawer is assembled and the glue has cured, sand and finish. Make the other drawers as necessary. The drawers do not touch each other or the cabinet and this allows the drawer fronts to be fitted after the drawers are in place. Carefully cut the required number of drawer fronts and check that they fit in place. Then fit the fronts to the drawers with double-sided tape and when their position is correct, fit the fronts to the drawers using screws from inside the drawer into the front. Fit one at a time to check that all remain in the correct position as they are fitted in place (Fig. 6c).

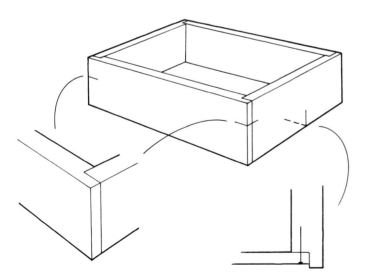

Fig. 7 Drawer made with simple lap joints

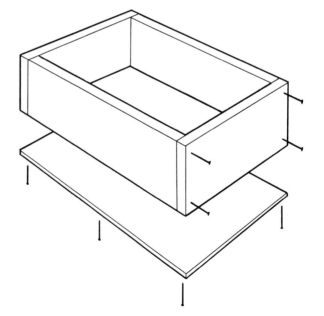

Fig. 8 Drawer made with butt joints

MANUFACTURED BOARD

Plywood is manufactured from sheets of timber veneer, the veneers being glued together with the grain of each lamination at right angles to the previous lamination. It is very good when used in thin sheets as backs of cabinets and drawer bottoms (Fig. 9a) In larger thicknesses (Fig. 9b), however, distortion is possible, particularly when the board is not restrained. Therefore, it is suitable for cabinets, but less suitable for doors.

Another good material for furniture-making uses solid timber as a core with veneers on the faces. This is called

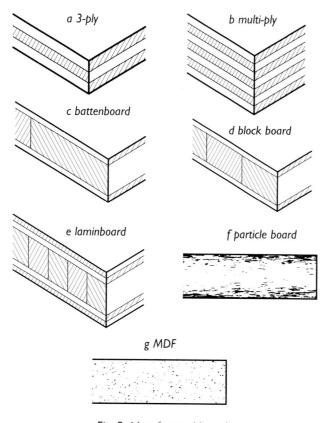

a 3-ply

b multi-ply

c battenboard

d block board

e laminboard

f particle board

g MDF

Fig. 9 Manufactured boards

batten board (Fig. 9c) when the internal timber is wide (1½–2 in, 38–51 mm), blockboard (Fig. 9d) when the core is ¾–1 inches (19 mm–25 mm) in thickness and laminboard (Fig. 9e) when the core is under ½ in (13mm). These boards are generally stable and would be used in high-quality furniture.

Particle board, or chipboard (Fig. 9) is timber which is reduced to chips which are then pressed into a density and thickness with bonding agents of modern synthetic adhesives. This board is very stable and has a good face for veneering, but you will find different qualities and densities. The major problem with chipboard is that it has a rough edge which needs to have a lipping applied because the structure means it is dense on the face but more open on the inside. It is therefore difficult to screw into the edge, particularly with the cheaper boards. The use of medium density fibreboard (Fig. 9) eliminates this edge problem. It can be cut, routed and shaped and the edges can be polished without the need for any lippings.

Take care with all manufactured boards in situations where there may be a high moisture level. With ply and blockboard, ensure that a waterproof adhesive has been used in the manufacture. Chipboard and MDF can be produced in waterproof grades. The use of these materials is suggested in many of the projects in the book, generally in cabinets where the structure holds all the panels into the cabinet shape and also where the finish to be applied is paint or lacquer. Pre-veneered boards are available and will help in the projects where you wish to have natural timber showing.

CUSTOMIZING

This project was made in a country style with a paint finish.

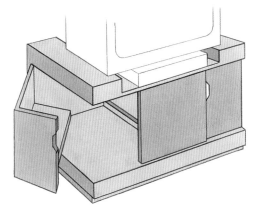

MODERN

I would prefer to use a timber finish for this piece but would not make it from solid timber since the slight movement across the grain would cause structural problems. Therefore, it would be better to make the piece in veneered manufactured board and lip the edges. You can either leave the veneer natural and put a clear lacquer finish on it or stain the door with a colour to fit in with your room before applying a protective lacquer coat.

REPRODUCTION

The approach to this piece should be based on the style of your existing furniture. As with other projects, I would suggest mahogany or walnut, but oak is another timber that is often used for old-style furniture. The drawing shows some chamfering and moulding around the top of the unit, the inclusion of a shaped base instead of a plinth and the use of brass fittings for handles.

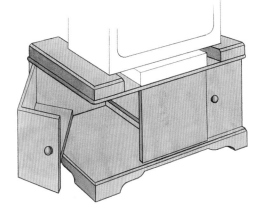

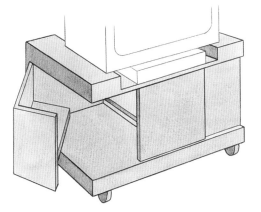

DESIGNER

Incorporating castors on this design will ensure that the unit can be moved easily. You might consider using a paint finish, possibly a matt black or grey that will match the colour of the TV and video units themselves. Another idea is to add handles made of brushed aluminium.

MATERIALS LIST: TV AND VIDEO UNIT (NOMINAL SIZES: IN/MM)

Item	Quantity	Length	Width	Thickness
Top & bottom (manufactured board)	2	23 in / 580 mm	18½ in / 470 mm	¾ in / 18 mm
Back (manufactured board)	1	22 in / 560 mm	18½ in / 464 mm	¾ in / 18 mm
Centre partition (manufactured board)	1	18½ in / 464 mm	17¼ in / 442 mm	¾ in / 18 mm
Front of plinth (manufactured board, mitred at 2 front corners)	1	22 in / 560 mm	4 in / 100 mm	⅝ in / 15 mm
Sides of plinth (manufactured board, mitred at 2 front corners)	2	18 in / 460 mm	4 in / 100 mm	⅝ in / 15 mm
Fixed centrefront	1	18½ in / 46 mm	10 in / 250 mm	¾/ 18 mm
Side doors (manufactured board. Dimension allows for mitre at front corner)	2	18½ in / 464 mm	17¼ / 442 mm	⅝ / 15 mm
Front of side doors (manufactured board. Dimension allows for mitre at front corner)	2	18½ in / 464 mm	6 in / 155 mm	⅝ in / 15 mm
Shelves per L-shaped door fixed to sides (manufactured board)	4	16½ in / 420 mm	4 in / 100 mm	⅝ in / 15 mm
Shelves in centre spaces (manufactured board)	2	16½ in / 420 mm	4 in / 100 mm	⅝ in / 15 mm
Lengths of piano hinge & screws	2	18 ¼ in / 460 mm		
Door catches	2			
TV support blocks (adjust distance between to suit video width & TV feet: this part can be made as a hollow box rather than solid block)	2	18 / 460 mm	4 in / 100 mm	2½ in / 65 mm

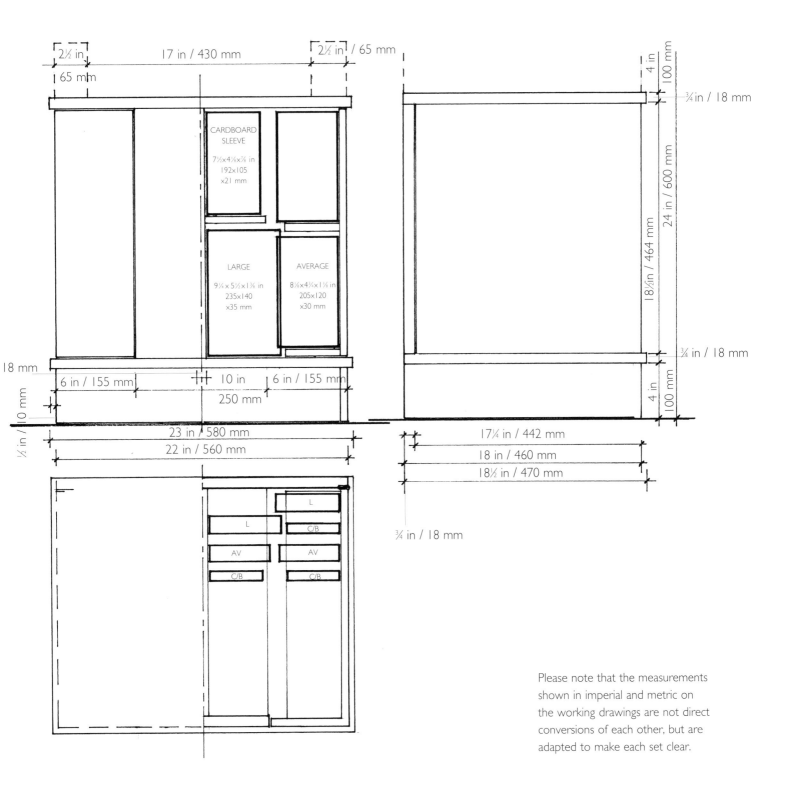

2½ in / 65 mm

17 in / 430 mm

2½ in / 65 mm

65 mm

4 in / 100 mm

¾ in / 18 mm

CARDBOARD
SLEEVE

7½ x 4⅛ x ⅞ in
192 x 105
x 21 mm

24 in / 600 mm

18½ in / 464 mm

LARGE

9¼ x 5½ x 1⅜ in
235 x 140
x 35 mm

AVERAGE

8⅛ x 4¾ x 1⅛ in
205 x 120
x 30 mm

¾ in / 18 mm

18 mm

6 in / 155 mm

10 in

6 in / 155 mm

250 mm

4 in / 100 mm

½ in / 10 mm

23 in / 580 mm

22 in / 560 mm

17¼ in / 442 mm

18 in / 460 mm

18½ in / 470 mm

L

L

C/B

AV

AV

C/B

C/B

¾ in / 18 mm

Please note that the measurements
shown in imperial and metric on
the working drawings are not direct
conversions of each other, but are
adapted to make each set clear.

HI-FI UNIT

This unit design has an open front so that the hi-fi equipment is on view and you can use a remote control to operate it.

Because of the wide range of equipment available and the disparity of shapes and sizes, you need to take careful measurements. Remember that as well as storing the components, you also need to connect cables between the units and to the power and speakers. Some units are made as a stacking system, but otherwise you will need to put in some intermediary shelves. I would recommend using adjustable shelving (see Bookcase, page 39). This design does not include speakers as they generally need to be sited separately.

MAKING SEQUENCE

1. Manufactured board has been used for the construction of this fairly simple unit. If you intend to paint the unit there is no problem with using screws and glue on the outside. If you use veneered board, you will have to make the joints with tongues, biscuits or dowels. It is possible to use solid wood but you will probably have to join narrow boards edge to edge to obtain the width. Also remember that the grain direction is important, since some of the components will have to be fixed in a way that allows for the difference in movement across and with the grain.

2. Mark out the back, the two internal sides and the shelf (Fig. 1). Then cut all the joints for fixing these components together and for fixing the other components to them.

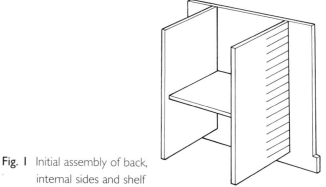

Fig. 1 Initial assembly of back, internal sides and shelf

3. Before assembly, cut the series of grooves in the rear outside face of the internal sides that will house the supports for the CDs (Fig. 2). The best machine for this task is the hand-held power router. It is practical to work the corresponding grooves on the inside face of the rear external sides at the same time, and then make and insert the CD support strips into these grooves.

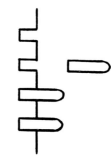

Fig. 2 The series of grooves are cut in the internal sides and in the rear external sides and the CD support slips are glued in position

4. Once you have glued the first stage and the glue has cured, you can apply the cabinet bottom and the rear external sides (Fig. 3 overleaf).

5. Let the glue cure and then apply the rear top batten onto which the hinged top will fit (Fig. 4) and then fit the plinth (Fig. 5). Your main structure is now finished.

6. Make the two front/side forward L-shaped doors by joining the corners with a mitre and cutting the grooves that will accept the five shelves (Fig. 6).

7. Cut each shelf accurately and square so that they ensure the L-shaped doors remain square. They will, in fact, act as reinforcements to the corner joint.

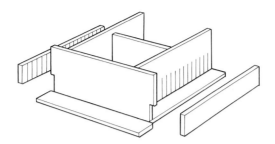

Fig. 3 Applying the cabinet bottom and the rear external sides

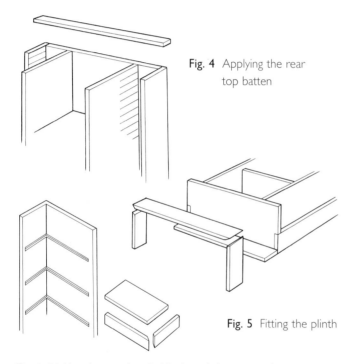

Fig. 4 Applying the rear top batten

Fig. 5 Fitting the plinth

Fig. 6 Making the two-handed L-shaped doors, together with the shelves for holding cassettes

8. Glue together the two sides and the five shelves, remembering that one will be left-handed and one right-handed. When the glue has cured, apply the small edge lippings. These can simply be glued to the shelf edges, or you can make grooves in them that will locate on to these edges.

9. Now make the hinged top and the small door for the front.

10. All the components should now be ready for final assembly to the main structure. First, hinge the two opening front doors, then the front door of the LP cabinet, and finally the hinged top (Fig. 7). You will probably then have to do some fine fitting. The cabinet work should now be completed.

11. Continue to prepare the surfaces for finishing and then apply your chosen finish.

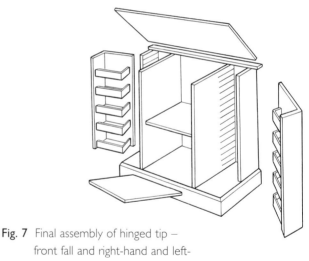

Fig. 7 Final assembly of hinged tip – front fall and right-hand and left-hand L-shaped doors

FINISHING

Whatever finish you decide to use, it is important to prepare the surface well. If you are planning to paint the wood, you can fill any blemishes with cellulose filler. Try to avoid damaging veneered board since it is difficult to fill blemishes in natural timber surfaces.

With a unit made of a natural timber you could use a finish to enhance its natural colour. Some of the dark timbers such as mahogany may need staining to make the colour more even. A stain may also be an effective feature for light-coloured woods. When using a stain, test it first on a scrap sample of the wood to check what effect it will have. On pieces made from solid natural timber you are likely to want a clear finish, but remember that the timber will darken over time.

Oil or wax can be used as natural finishes, but do not give the thorough protection of lacquers and varnishes.

Oil finishes
The advantage of using oil is that a surface can easily be sanded and re-oiled after damage.

Linseed oil
Raw linseed oil takes some time to dry, while the boiled variety dries more quickly.

Tung oil
This is the most durable oil finish and is fairly resistant.

Danish and teak oils
These have a short drying time and need to be applied in a series of thin coats.

Wax finishes
You can either use natural preparations such as beeswax or carnauba, or the many ready-made preparations available. Applying wax with some fine wire wool to the finished surface gives an effective matt finish quality. Wax should be combined with other finishes to give a durable result.

Natural finishes
Before the development of chemical lacquers, finishes were based on shellac. Shellac (also called French polish) can be bought as button polish which is golden brown in colour, garnet polish which is dark red-brown and used for darker timbers, white polish made from bleached shellac for lighter woods or transparent polish for very pale timbers. The polish is applied with a brush, each coat is allowed to dry and then rubbed down lightly between coats with silicon carbide paper.

Laquer finishes
One of the more traditional lacquers is nitro cellulose lacquer, which dries by the evaporation of solvents. There are two different types of lacquers made with modern synthetic resins. In one the lacquer is mixed with a catalyst which only starts to cure when it is applied to the work and exposed to the air. In others mixing a separate lacquer and catalyst gives a preparation that will set with the chemical reaction. You only have a short time to apply these finishes. For the greatest protection use the latter type but either will give you a good finish.

Other finishes
If you plan to paint your piece, most decorating paints can be used. If you wish to decorate the surface you can use decorating emulsion paints and add a couple of coats of clear one or two pack catalysed lacquer.

Wax

Matt 2 pack PU

Gloss 1 pack gloss

Oil

2 pack PU wire wood and wax sanded

CUSTOMIZING

The piece is shown in a country style which allows the hi-fi equipment to be seen. This also means that remote controls may be easily used. The other options are shown with fronts that cover the equipment, but in all cases the central doors may be omitted if you wish it to be on view. The tops only need to open if an LP record deck is part of the system.

REPRODUCTION

This version will again use a dark wood. You should be able to use manufactured board with appropriate veneers. The base has the plinth cut as shown to indicate traditional feet and a moulding can be applied to the top edge. The front doors are hinged and you can use brass fittings to complete the effect.

MODERN

Use simple, light timbers for this option. The plinth is set back from the main cupboard structure and the front-opening sides have their tops level with the main lid.

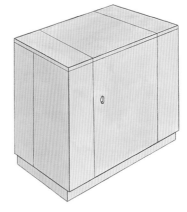

DESIGNER

This is similar to the modern version, but it is envisaged that this option could use interesting painted features. You could use bright and contrast paint finishes or metallic paints, or choose subtle colours and add stencils or other types of decoration.

MATERIALS LIST: HI-FI UNIT (NOMINAL SIZES: IN/MM)

Item	Quantity	Length	Width	Thickness
Back	1	36 in / 920 mm	27 in / 685 mm	¾ in / 18 mm
Internal sides	2	32 in / 820 mm	15¼ in / 390 mm	¾ in / 18 mm
Shelf	1	15 in / 375 mm	14 in / 350 mm	¾ in / 18 mm
Bottom	1	27 in / 685 mm	15¼ in / 390 mm	¾ in / 18 mm
Outside uprights	2	32 in / 820 mm	6½ in / 168 mm	¾ in / 18 mm
Plinth front	1	28 in / 710 mm	4 in / 100 mm	¾ in / 18 mm
Plinth sides	2	16½ in / 423 mm	4 in / 100 mm	¾ in / 18 mm
Rear top batten (could be solid timber)	1	28 in / 710 mm	1½ in / 35 mm	1 in / 25 mm
Top	1	28 in / 710 mm	15 in / 380 mm	1 in / 25 mm
Door	1	14 in / 350 mm	13¼ in / 340 mm	¾ in / 18 mm
L-shaped doors (sides)	2	32 in / 820 mm	10 in / 240 mm	¾ in / 18 mm
L-shaped doors (fronts, allowance made for mitres on front corners)	2	32 in / 820 mm	5¾ in / 147 mm	¾ in / 18 mm
L-shaped doors (shelves, allowance made for mitres on front corners)	10	8¾ in / 220 mm	2¾ in / 70 mm	½in / 12 mm
Edge lippings to shelves (to make both long & short sides)	10	13 in / 320 mm	1 in / 25 mm	⅜ in / 10 mm
2 butts per hinged edge or 1 piano per hinged edge & screws as necessary				

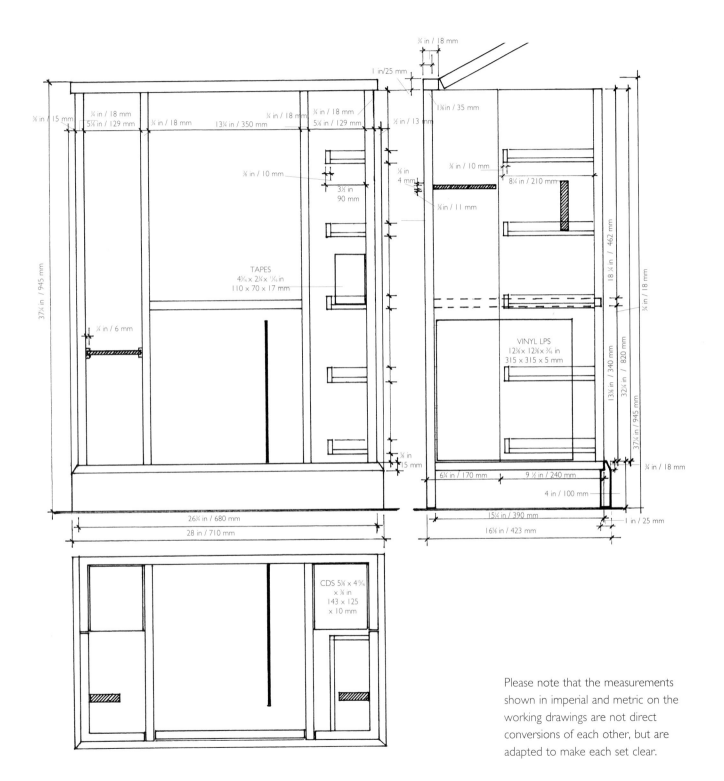

TAPES
4⅜ × 2¾ × ¹¹⁄₁₆ in
110 × 70 × 17 mm

VINYL LPS
12⅜ × 12⅜ × ³⁄₁₆ in
315 × 315 × 5 mm

CDS 5⅝ × 4¹⁵⁄₁₆
× ⅜ in
143 × 125
× 10 mm

Please note that the measurements
shown in imperial and metric on the
working drawings are not direct
conversions of each other, but are
adapted to make each set clear.

DROP-LEAF TABLE

This style of table is useful for use in a restricted space, because it takes up little space but can unfold to seat a reasonable number of people. If you are particularly short of space this design also has the advantage of allowing items to be stored inside the main frame when the tops are closed. Both solid wood and manufactured board can be used.

MAKING SEQUENCE

1. Prepare all the components and cut them to size (a main frame, four gates, one top and two drop leaves). The main frame (Fig. 1) is composed of two ends, one

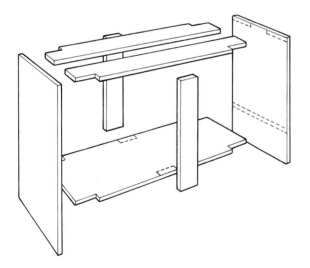

Fig. 1   Components needed for the main frame

bottom cross rail, two top cross rails and two vertical stiles. Solid timber should be used for the two top rails and the vertical stiles but the two ends and the bottom cross rail could be made from manufactured board.

Mark out on the inside of the ends where the three cross rails will join and then mark the end of the bottom rail and the two top rails. Remember to cut out the ends of these pieces.

2. The joints for these rails can now be made. If you are using solid wood throughout, tenon the bottom cross rail into the sides and use lap dovetails between the two top rails and the top of the sides (Fig. 2). If you are using manufactured board for the three components, it may be better to use tongue and groove, biscuits or dowels.

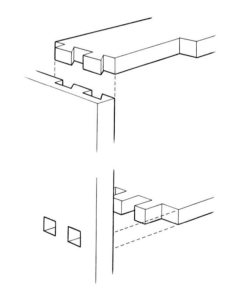

Fig. 2   The top rails are lap dovetailed and the bottom rails tenoned into the sides

3. Assemble the rails dry, mark the two vertical stiles that will go between them to the correct dimension and then make the joints. Always use tenons for solid wood, but with manufactured board any alternatives can be used.

4. Mask the joint surfaces and sand the components. It is a good idea to finish everything at this stage except the outsides of the two ends. When this finish is dry, glue the whole assembly together. Then prepare the materials for the four gates (all the joints would be mortise and tenons for solid timber), marking carefully and checking from the already assembled main frame.

5. Fit all joints dry and check for size and square (see page 16). Assemble these four frames (Fig. 3). Fit the edges between the gates and the vertical stiles in the main frame.

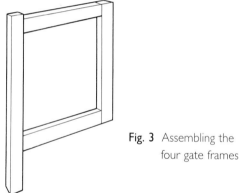

Fig. 3 Assembling the four gate frames

6. The hinges will have to be fitted carefully so that the long stile of the gate which makes the leg fits into the correct position when opened (Fig. 4). The hinge may have to be adjusted to ensure a good fit. When the hinging is correct, remove the gates, finish the components and refix.

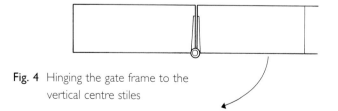

Fig. 4 Hinging the gate frame to the vertical centre stiles

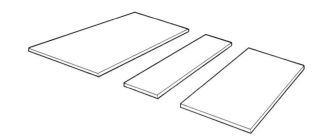

Fig. 5 The narrow centre top and the two folding leaves

7. Make the top and the two drop leaves. Mark the narrow centre top and the wider leaves (Fig. 5) and shape the joining edges. Use either a ruled joint, as shown in the working drawing, or a mitre joint. If solid timber is used, the ruled joint is simple to make and if you have a router there are cutters available which will assist the process. If manufactured board is used, it will need lipping. With pre-veneered board, the lipping will be visible on the face. The making, lipping and veneering of the three tops are not recommended unless you have some experience of this process.

The mitred edge is simple to make (Fig. 6), but the knuckle of the hinge will show on the folding edges and you may need to drill extra holes or fit larger hinges to give the screws enough material to bite securely.

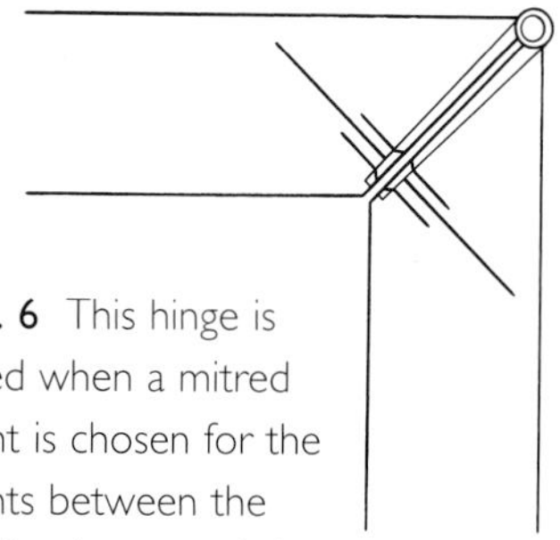

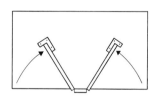

Fig. 6 This hinge is used when a mitred joint is chosen for the joints between the folding leaves and the fixed central top

Fig. 7 Gate stops are fitted underneath the drop leaves to ensure that support is in the correct place

8. Fit the hinges and, having checked that they are fitted correctly, attach the top on to the bottom frame and check that the gates support the two drop leaves.

9. Gate stops (Fig. 7), which allow the gates to be opened to the optimum position, will need to be fitted underneath these top leaves to ensure that the gates are in the correct position when opened.

10. Remove the top from the frame along with the hinges. Sand and finish all the pieces, reassemble them and complete any final finishing.

TIP

SAWING TENONS

The instructions below should help the accurate sawing of a tenon. The method of marking out a mortise and tenon is shown on p.17.

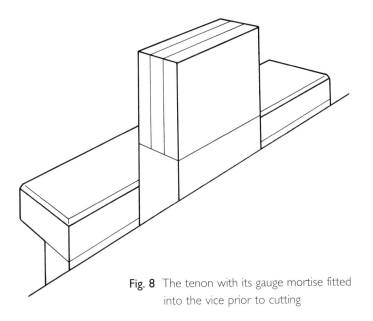

Fig. 8 The tenon with its gauge mortise fitted into the vice prior to cutting

Mark the tenon with a gauge mark, and the shoulders with a knife. Place the tenon in the vice (Fig. 8) and make the series of cuts shown in Fig. 9.

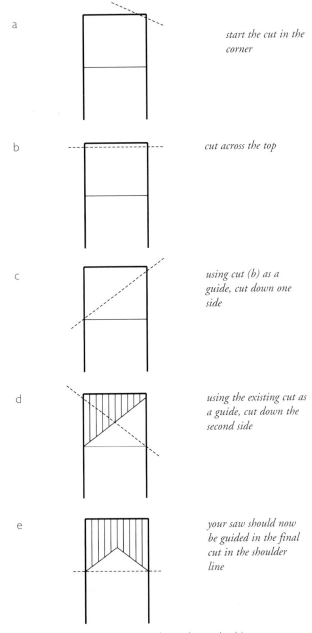

a — *start the cut in the corner*

b — *cut across the top*

c — *using cut (b) as a guide, cut down one side*

d — *using the existing cut as a guide, cut down the second side*

e — *your saw should now be guided in the final cut in the shoulder line*

Figs 9 A series of cuts are made as shown in this sequence

CUSTOMIZING

COUNTRY

This could be made in a light timber, either in pine or one of the hardwoods such as beech, ash, sycamore or maple. It is important to ensure that you match the grain of the two drop leaves and the fixed central portion, since when both leaves are open the piece will look much better if the top pattern appears to have been selected. You can also add features that reflect the country feel by adding a cross batten to the bottom of the sides and by bringing the bottom shelf through the side and pegging it, as shown in the drawing.

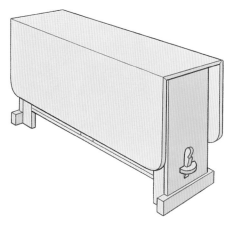

REPRODUCTION

This look can be achieved by using darker woods such as walnut or mahogany. The side leaves can have fairly large rounds on the corners so that when opened the top is a rectangle with four curved corners. You can also increase the effect by shaping the ends, using the design as shown in the drawing, or making a shape that is suitable and that matches your other furniture.

DESIGNER

This piece has the elements divided into smaller rectangles or squares, with exotic veneers such as bird's-eye maple or burr elm/walnut. These will give a very interesting grain effect. Choose one of these if you have had some experience with veneering, or achieve a similar effect by using different-coloured paints.

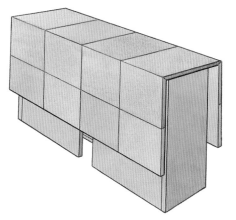

MATERIALS LIST: DROP LEAF TABLE (NOMINAL SIZES: IN/MM)				
Item	Quantity	Length	Width	Thickness
Ends to U/frame	2	27¼ in / 680 mm	8½ in / 210 mm	1 in / 25 mm
Top cross rails (total width cut to shoulder length if not using mortise & tenon joints)	2	26 in / 660 mm	2½ in / 60 mm	¾ in / 20 mm
Bottom cross rail (total width cut to shoulder length if not using mortise & tenon joints)	1	26 in / 660 mm	10 in / 250 mm	¾ in / 20 mm
Centre uprights	2	17¾ in / 440 mm	2 in / 50 mm	¾ in / 20 mm
Opening gates (legs)	4	27¼ in / 680 mm	2½ in / 60 mm	¾ in / 20 mm
Opening gates (centre stiles)	4	17¾ in / 440 mm	2½ in / 60 mm	¾ in / 20 mm
Opening gates (all cross rails at shoulders. Allow extra for joints of mortise & tenon)	8	7 in / 185 mm	2½ in / 60 mm	¾ in / 20 mm
Top	1	30 in / 760 mm	12 in / 300 mm	¾ in / 20 mm
Side drop leaves	2	30 in / 760 mm	16 in / 4000 mm	¾ in / 20 mm
Hinges for 4 gates (8 butts, 4 piano, or make own pivot hinge and screws to match				
Hinges between top & 2 drop leaves (see alternatives: 1. Long hinges on mitre; 2. Brass butts on closing edges; 3. Backflap hinges on rule joint.)				

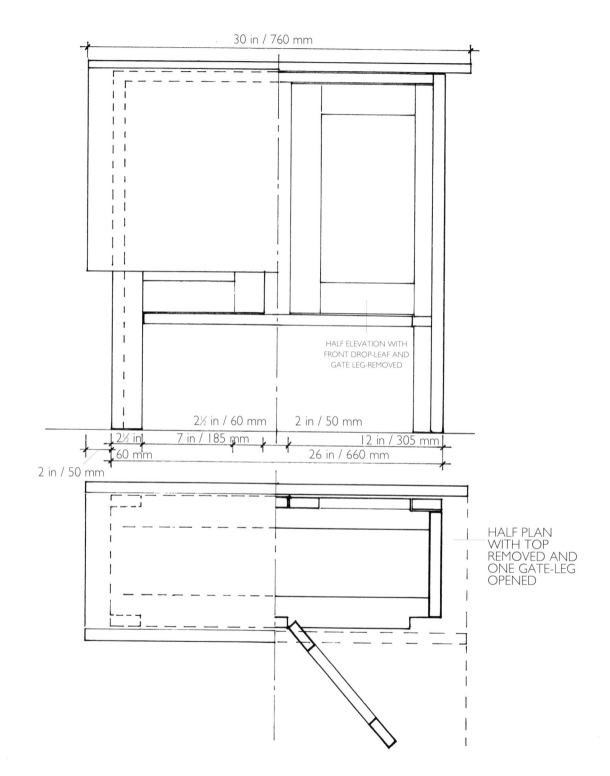

30 in / 760 mm

HALF ELEVATION WITH
FRONT DROP-LEAF AND
GATE LEG-REMOVED

2½ in / 60 mm   2 in / 50 mm

2½ in   7 in / 185 mm   12 in / 305 mm

60 mm   26 in / 660 mm

2 in / 50 mm

HALF PLAN
WITH TOP
REMOVED AND
ONE GATE-LEG
OPENED

DROP-LEAF TABLE

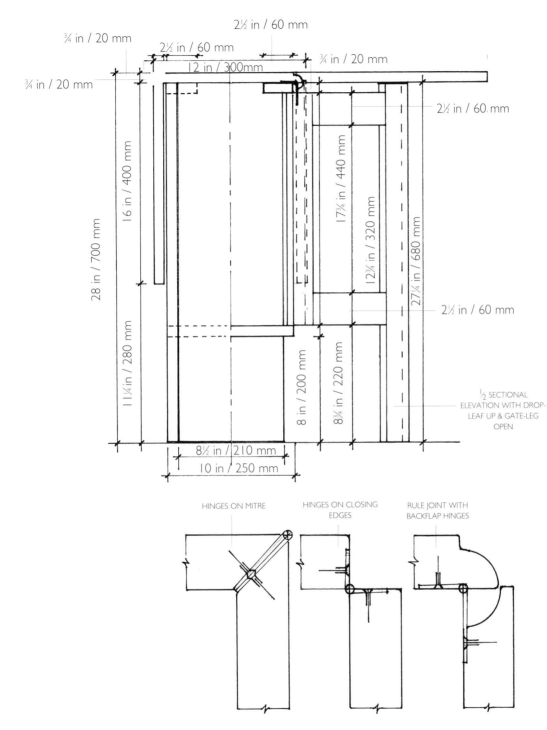

¾ in / 20 mm

2½ in / 60 mm

2½ in / 60 mm

¾ in / 20 mm

12 in / 300mm

¾ in / 20 mm

2½ in / 60 mm

16 in / 400 mm

17¾ in / 440 mm

12¾ in / 320 mm

27¼ in / 680 mm

28 in / 700 mm

2½ in / 60 mm

11¼ in / 280 mm

8 in / 200 mm

8¾ in / 220 mm

½ SECTIONAL ELEVATION WITH DROP-LEAF UP & GATE-LEG OPEN

8½ in / 210 mm

10 in / 250 mm

HINGES ON MITRE

HINGES ON CLOSING EDGES

RULE JOINT WITH BACKFLAP HINGES

Please note that the measurements shown in imperial and metric on the working drawings are not direct conversions of each other, but are adapted to make each set clear.

CORNER CUPBOARD

The construction of this piece, like others in this book, is simplified when the work is broken down into components. This has been made in the reproduction style and although it may look complicated, the component nature of the structure should ensure that making up is relatively easy. The cabinet is made first, then the front frame and door and then the styling features.

MAKING SEQUENCE

1. The cabinet is made from manufactured board, using two sides, a top, a bottom and a back surface (Fig. 1). First of all, mark out and cut these components to size.

2. Assemble the cabinet with screws and glue (tongues, biscuits or dowels can be used in addition). Screws can

be used here as they will be hidden against the wall. Here, a back strip has been added to flatten off the corner. This is often better for the interior of the cabinet and gives an effective way of mounting the cabinet on the wall. Remember that wall corners are not always square and flat and any irregularities must be accounted for.

3. After assembling the cabinet, finish the inside and outside and mask the front face on to which the frame will fit. You can now decide whether to have fixed or adjustable shelving.

4. Make the front frame using joints with simple mortise and tenons (Fig. 2). Assemble it dry and check its position on the face of the cabinet.

Fig. 2 Making the front frame

Glue the frame and when it is dry, cut the bevel on the rear edges and fix the frame to the front of the cabinet with screws from behind. Make sure that there is a gap between the sides of the frames and the walls. This is so that the irregular shadow line which is created between the cabinet and the wall where it is not even does not

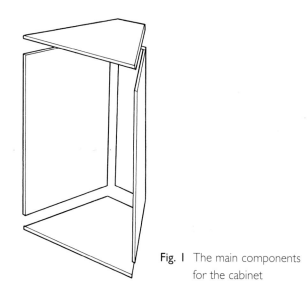

Fig. 1 The main components for the cabinet

make the cabinet look crooked. Scribing (matching the frame edge exactly to the shape of the wall) is inadvisable, as it will probably disturb the balance of the front by turning the vertical parallel frame stiles into ones with uneven wavy edges.

5. Make the door (Fig. 3) using mortise and tenons and, as it will be glazed, make an internal rebate on the inside edges so that the glass can be inserted from the inside.

Fig. 3 Part of the door showing the rebates into which the glass will be set from the inside

Once assembled, check that it fits in the frame, apply the hinges and then fit the closing side and the handle. When it fits, remove the door temporarily from the frame since it will be easier to apply the period features without it in position.

6. Apply the bottom feature first. This is a simple cross-rail which can be slightly shaped on the bottom (Fig. 4), but be careful not to overdo the shaping. The ends should be mitred from the rear so that after the sharp edge is removed the shadow line against the wall is similar to that of the frame. Fix it from the inside of the front frame with screws and glue.

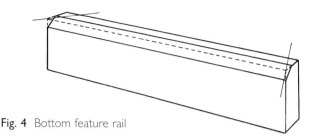

Fig. 4 Bottom feature rail

7. The top rail should now be cut and made. Size the groove on the front to accept the cockbead (Fig. 5c). Make the cockbead (Fig. 5d) by cutting and planing to size and rounding the front edge. Insert in the groove. Then make the L-section top strip (Fig. 5b) and glue it in place. Cut a series of small blocks to the measurements shown on the technical drawing and glue them in place (Fig. 5e). You can now cut the rail to length with mitres at each end and fix it to the frame in the same way as the bottom rail.

8. Make the curved feature (Fig. 5a) for the top of the cupboard and position it centrally. Then sand and finish all the components and make the batten that fixes into the corner that will hold the cabinet.

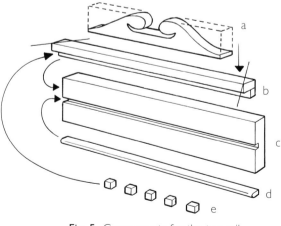

Fig. 5 Components for the top rail

9. You now need to decide on the final finish for the door. The door shown is glazed, but you can also use veneered panels. If you decide to use glass, make sure it has bevelled edges or glazing bars. The simplest method of glazing the door is to cut fine bars yourself from wood and fit and glue to the surface with wood-to-glass glue as here. If you are a skilled woodworker, however, you can make timber bars and fit the glass in them. Otherwise you can ask your glazier if he could apply lead strips. Remember that for safety all glass should be toughened.

VENEER

Veneer is made from thin sheets of timber which are cut from timber logs. When making veneer for plywood, the veneer is peeled in large sheets from the log as it is turned slowly. When used for decorative purposes, the face veneers are sliced from a balk of timber which can be produced radially or tangentially to maximize the natural grain of the timber. Decorative veneers are usually laid on a manufactured board base and this industrial process uses large presses and special adhesives. It can be laid by hand using animal glues, but this technique is now only used for restoration and specialist work. It is generally advisable to use pre-veneered board.

The most practical way of veneering by hand is on relatively small components. You must ensure that you can apply pressure to all parts of the surface from the centre to the outside with G-cramps.

1. Cut the veneer (Fig. 6a) slightly oversize to cover both sides of the surface.

2. Then cut two thickish pieces of manufactured board (Fig. 6b) (known as cauls) that are slightly larger than both the surface and the cut veneer.

3. Apply adhesive between the veneer and the surface to be veneered. Place a sheet of polythene (Fig. 6c) between the veneer and the caul (the polythene and the caul together will protect the veneer, which is extremely thin and fragile) and apply cramps (Fig. 7), making sure that the veneer does not slip out of position as you apply the cramp pressure.

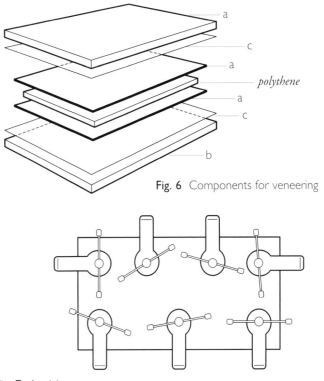

Fig. 6 Components for veneering

Fig. 7 Applying cramps

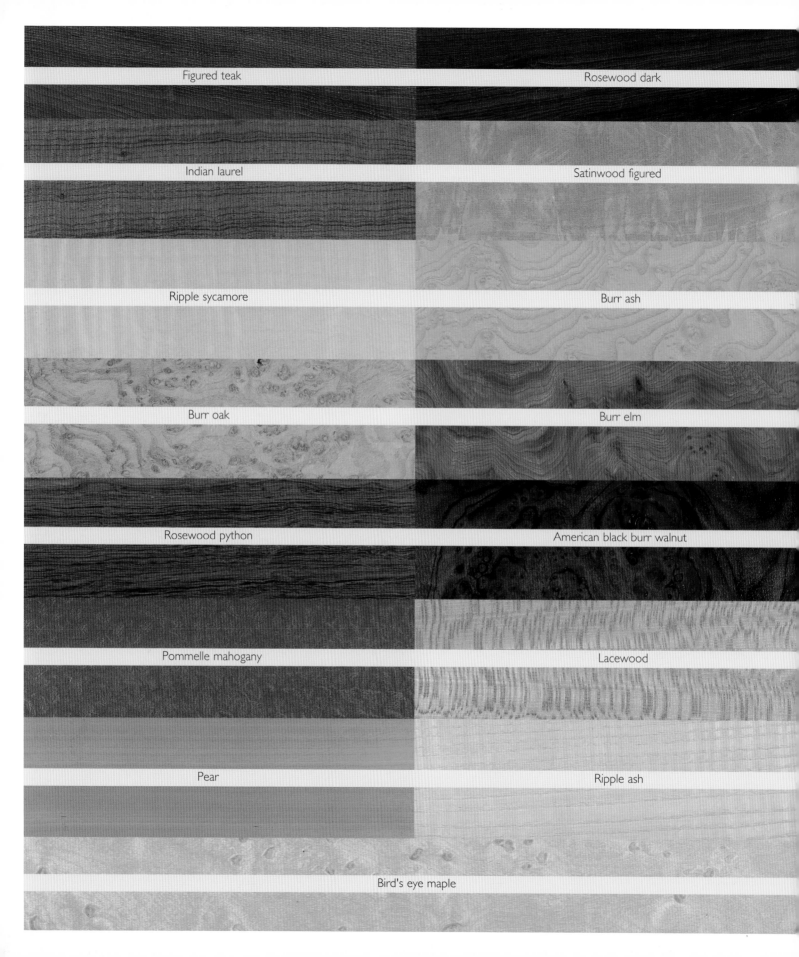

Figured teak

Rosewood dark

Indian laurel

Satinwood figured

Ripple sycamore

Burr ash

Burr oak

Burr elm

Rosewood python

American black burr walnut

Pommelle mahogany

Lacewood

Pear

Ripple ash

Bird's eye maple

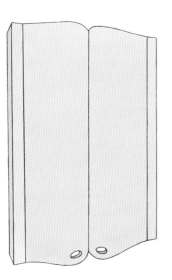

The version photographed was made in a reproduction style, but alternatives will look much simpler.

COUNTRY

This option could simply use two doors made of solid timber or with an interesting veneer. As drawn, the doors are shaped to emphasize the centre opening line, while the curve on the bottom has holes drilled for handles. You will need to select your timber or veneer very carefully, since the final effect will depend on that choice.

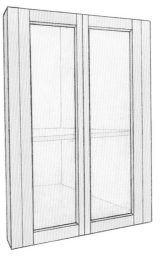

MODERN

This uses two simple doors which are 'planted' onto the face. Interest will be given by the choice of timber, together with the contrasting line that runs around the glazed openings. As well as using ordinary clear glass, you can change the effect by using frosted or tinted glass, or use a form of metal mesh.

DESIGNER

This version uses tongue and groove boarding for the door, but instead of fixing this horizontally or vertically, it is arranged to give a 'V' effect. You can emphasize this by angling the tops and bottoms of each door, giving an upward or downward pointing chevron. The effect can be further highlighted by colouring the surfaces of the tongue and groove chamfers.

MATERIALS LIST: CORNER CUPBOARD (NOMINAL SIZES: IN/MM)				
Item	*Quantity*	*Length*	*Width*	*Thickness*
Top & bottom of carcass (ply or manufactured board)	2	16 in / 400 mm	6½ in / 165 mm	⅝ in / 15 mm
Sides of carcass	2	19½ in / 490 mm	9⅝ in / 235 mm	⅝ in / 15 mm
Back of carcass	1	19½ in / 490 mm	4 in / 100 mm	¾ in / 20 mm
Vertical triangular mounting for batten	1	18 in / 460 mm	2⅞ in / 70 mm	1½ in / 40 mm
Main front frame (2 stiles)	2	24 in / 600 mm	2⅞ in / 70 mm	¾ in / 20 mm
Main front frame Upper and lower cross rails. (Add extra to length for mortise & tenon joints)	2	12 in / 300 mm	2 in / 50 mm	¾ in / 20 mm
Door frame (2 stiles)	2	17½ in / 440 mm	1½ in / 40 mm	¾ in / 20 mm
Door frame (top rail. Add extra to length if mortise & tenon joints)	1	9 in / 220 mm	1½ in / 40 mm	¾ in / 20 mm
Door frame (bottom rail. Add extra to length if mortise & tenon joints)	1	9 in / 220 mm	2 in / 50 mm	¾ in / 20 mm
Bottom cross rail	1	18¾ in / 470 mm	2¾ in / 70 mm	¾ in / 20 mm
Top detail (top rail)	1	20 in / 500 mm	3¾ in / 90 mm	¾ in / 20 mm
Top detail (cockbead)	1	20 in / 500 mm	½ in / 12 mm	3/16 in / 5 mm
Top detail (L-section)	1	20 in / 500 mm	1¾ in / 38 mm	⅞ in / 15 mm
Top detail (small blocks. Cut strip 20 in (500 mm) ½ in × ¼ in, and cut series of single pieces)	25	⅝ in / 15 mm	½ in / 12 mm	¼ in / 5 mm
Top detail (top curved shape)	1	12 in / 300 mm	2¼ in / 55 mm	¾ in / 20 mm
Glass (glazing bar effect, engraved on glass or wood stripes)	1	14¾ in / 360 mm	9¾ in / 250 mm	3/16 in / 4 mm
Hinges plus screws	2 decorative			
Door catch	1 decorative			

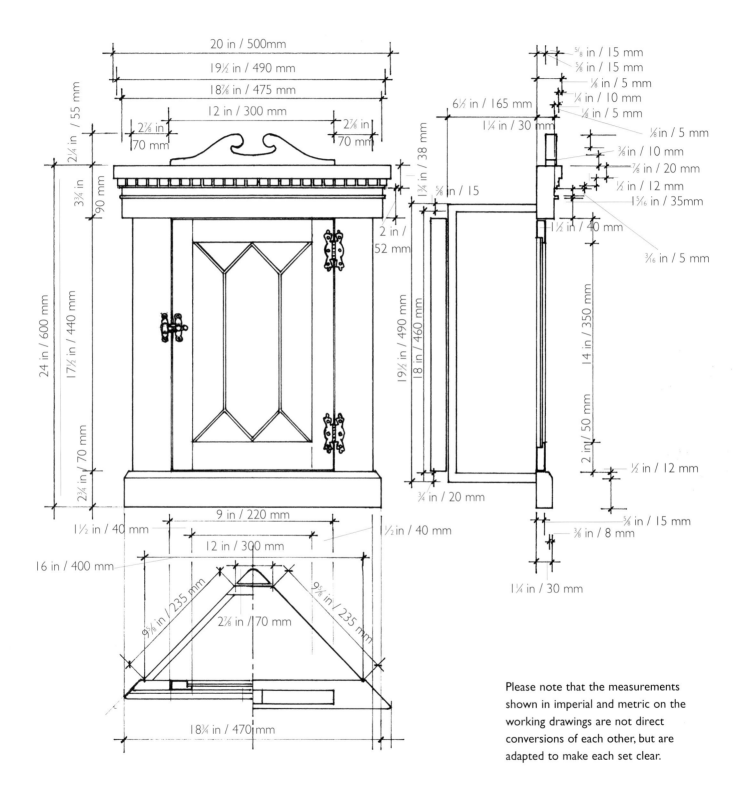

20 in / 500mm
19½ in / 490 mm
18⅞ in / 475 mm
12 in / 300 mm
2⅞ in / 70 mm
2⅞ in / 70 mm
2¼ in / 55 mm
3¾ in / 90 mm
2 in / 52 mm
24 in / 600 mm
17½ in / 440 mm
2¾ in / 70 mm

9 in / 220 mm
1½ / 40 mm
½ in / 40 mm
12 in / 300 mm
16 in / 400 mm
9⅝ in / 235 mm
9⅝ in / 235 mm
2⅞ in / 70 mm
18¾ in / 470 mm

6½ in / 165 mm
1¼ in / 30 mm
⅝ in / 15 mm
⅝ in / 15 mm
⅛ in / 5 mm
¼ in / 10 mm
⅛ in / 5 mm
⅛ in / 5 mm
⅜ in / 10 mm
⅞ in / 20 mm
½ in / 12 mm
1⁵⁄₁₆ in / 35mm
3⁄16 in / 5 mm
1½ in / 40 mm
1¾ in / 38 mm
⅝ in / 15
19½ in / 490 mm
18 in / 460 mm
14 in / 350 mm
2 in / 50 mm
½ in / 12 mm
⅝ in / 15 mm
⅜ in / 8 mm
1¼ in / 30 mm
¾ in / 20 mm

Please note that the measurements shown in imperial and metric on the working drawings are not direct conversions of each other, but are adapted to make each set clear.

SEWING BOX

This piece has been designed to carry a compact collection of sewing and needlework materials. However, you can redesign the space division to suit individual needs. The cabinet can be scaled up to allow extra storage space and this will require the alteration of the triangle, the height of the box and the number and size of shelves. Wheels or castors could also be added.

MAKING SEQUENCE

1. Start by marking out the back of the box (Fig. 1). You will need to decide whether you wish to use wheels or castors, as this will alter the position of the bottom in relation to the back. If you have chosen wheels, cut the spaces for them. If you are using castors that will be fixed to the underside back corner of the triangular bottom, make the necessary allowances.

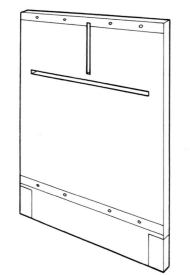

Fig. 1 Marking out the back of the box, showing the position of the two triangular tops and bottoms, the grooves for the web band top fixed shelf, and the cut outs needed for the castors or wheels

2. Mark the two triangular tops and bottoms and make the joint to fix them to the back (Fig. 2). In this example a mitre has been used with a loose tongue, but a single or double lap joint would be as suitable. The top has been fitted to the front of the back, but it could be made as a slightly larger triangle and fitted on the top of the back itself.

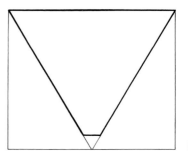

Fig. 2 Triangular top

3. With these three components dry-jointed, make the front stile, starting with a rectangular section and reducing this to a triangle (Fig. 3) by sawing and planing.

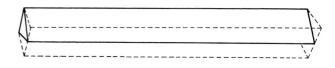

Fig. 3 Triangular front stile cut from a rectangular piece

4. Make the joints between the stile and the tops and bottoms. Small mortises and tenons have been used here. Mark and cut the pieces for the fixed internal shelves. Only two sides are needed for the deep bottom one, while two sides and a thin ply bottom are needed for the top (Fig. 4).

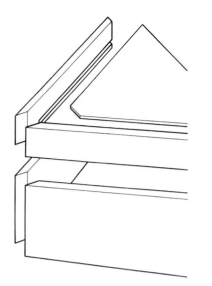

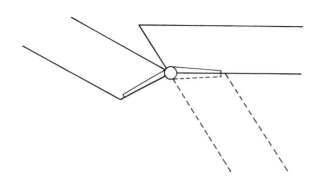

Fig. 5 The position of the piano hinge between the door and the triangular cabinet

Fig. 4 The internal shelves

5. Cut these slightly oversize to be finally fitted after the main carcass is assembled. In the diagram shown, in order to ensure that the unit stays square, a small web or gusset has been put on the inside between the top and back at the centre.

6. Now assemble the back and triangular top of the main carcass (see Tip opposite).

7. Fit the handle detail on the top of the front stile. A sphere purchased from a joinery supplier who makes staircases has been used here. If you have some experience of turning you could make your own.

8. Now make the two doors (Fig. 5). The photograph shows the use of butt hinges, but you could use a piano hinge as shown here since it is neat and gives several screw positions for fixing.

9. With the door hinged in place, make the four shelves (two for each door) and after checking the clearance, fit them in place (Fig. 6). The whole piece can now be smoothed, finished and the castors or wheels added.

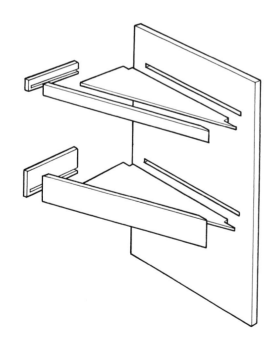

Fig. 6 Fitting the shelves onto the doors

TIP

ASSEMBLING TRIANGULAR SHAPES

It is not always easy to assemble triangular shapes, but with planning and care you should have few problems. Remember to try the assembly dry first. It is easier to insert the web when joining the triangular top to the back.

There are three ways of assembling the triangular top and the back (Figs. 7a–c):

a) Fix the top to the back from above. This will mean that the cramps will need to be located so as to give pressure as shown.

b) Fix the top to the back from the front, which will mean that a special cramping block will need to be made as shown.

c) Using mitres, blocks will need to be glued to the surface so that G-cramps can be used to tighten the joint.

When the web is in place, the two components are square and the glue has cured, prepare to assemble the bottom and front stile. Place the back on some supports and cramp as shown – you will need to make special cramping blocks to fit around the triangular stile (Fig. 8). Another pair of hands will help to keep the cramps steady in this assembly operation.

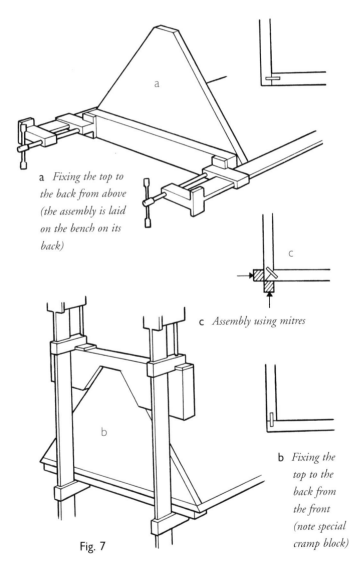

a *Fixing the top to the back from above (the assembly is laid on the bench on its back)*

c *Assembly using mitres*

b *Fixing the top to the back from the front (note special cramp block)*

Fig. 7

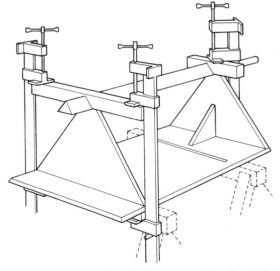

Fig. 8 Cramping the triangular bottom and the front stile

103

CUSTOMIZING

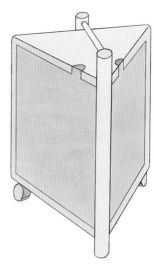

The unit as made took on a 'designer' style, contrasting natural timber with subtle flat colour.

COUNTRY

This can be approached using natural-looking timber or more lively colours. If you wish to use a natural timber effect, this would be best achieved by using veneered board and applying solid wood lippings, since the project is less suitable for construction in solid timber due to timber movement. The drawing shows a rounded front upright, with a top handle instead of a ball. The cabinet can have a degree of rounding on the hard edges and the door handles can protrude into the top.

REPRODUCTION

This option should use darker timbers or colours. Add character by using an interesting pattern on the doors and again using a top handle. Choose any fittings, e.g. handles, wheels, castors, to match your existing furniture.

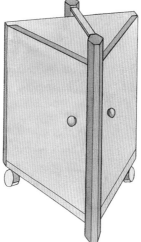

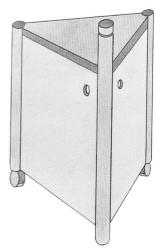

MODERN

This version would be in light timbers, but here the suggestion is that the front upright is rounded and this feature is also added to the two rear corners. To develop this approach, the castors fit below the rear uprights and the front one is extended to give a handle. The top will overhang the doors, while the handle will be simple holes.

MATERIALS LIST: SEWING BOX (NOMINAL SIZES: IN/MM)

Item	Quantity	Length	Width	Thickness
Back	1	24 in / 600 mm	16 in / 400 mm	1 in / 25 mm
Top/bottom (manufactured board. To be cut triangular)	2	16 in / 400 mm	11¾ in / 290 mm	¾ in /18 mm
Front upright (solid timber)	1	33 in / 825 mm	2½ in / 65 mm	2⅜ in / 35 mm
Web/gusset (plywood)	1	6 in / 150 mm	6 in / 150 mm	½ in / 12 mm
Doors (manufactured board)	2	19½ in / 485 mm	13 in / 325 mm	¾ in / 15 mm
Fitted into carcass top shelf (plywood. To be cut triangular)	1	13 in / 325 mm	10 in / 250 mm	¼ in / 6 mm
Fitted into carcass top shelf rails (solid timber)	2	13 in / 325 mm	2½ in / 60 mm	½ in / 12 mm
Fitted into carcass bottom rails (solid timber)	2	13 in / 325 mm	6 in / 150 mm	½ in / 12 mm
Door shelves (plywood. To be cut triangular)	4	12 in / 300 mm	9 in / 130 mm	¼ in / 6 mm
Door shelves top rails (solid timber. To make the 2 sides, cut 2 lengths to 17 in and make final cuts when making)	4	10½ in / 260 mm & 6 in / 150 mm	2¼ in / 55 mm	½ in /12 mm
Door shelves bottom rails (solid timber. To make the 2 sides, cut 2 lengths to 17 in (432 mm) and make final cuts when making)	4	10½ in / 260 mm & 4 in / 150 mm	4 in / 100 mm	½ in / 12 mm
Sphere	1	approx. 3 in (75 mm) diameter		
Wheels	2	approx. 2¾ in (70 mm) diameter		
Hinges (either 2 butts or 1 piano each side plus screws)	2			

Please note that the
measurements shown in
imperial and metric on the
working drawings are not
direct conversions of each
other, but are adapted to
make each set clear.

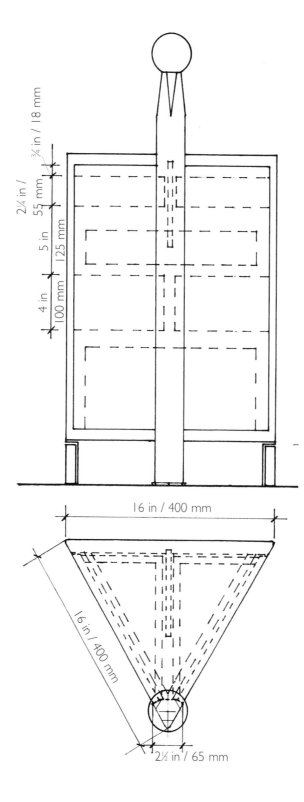

¾ in / 18 mm

2¼ in / 55 mm

5 in / 125 mm

4 in / 100 mm

16 in / 400 mm

16 in / 400 mm

2½ in / 65 mm

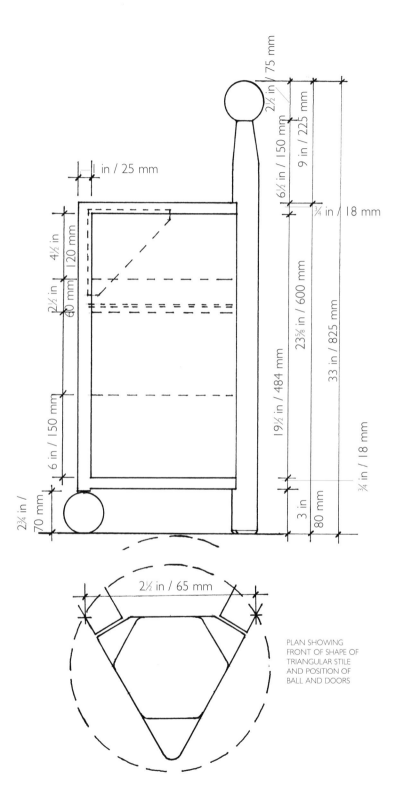

1 in / 25 mm

2½ in / 75 mm

9 in / 225 mm

6½ in / 150 mm

¾ in / 18 mm

4½ in / 120 mm

2½ in / 60 mm

23⅝ in / 600 mm

33 in / 825 mm

19½ in / 484 mm

6 in / 150 mm

¾ in / 18 mm

2¾ in / 70 mm

3 in / 80 mm

2½ in / 65 mm

PLAN SHOWING
FRONT OF SHAPE OF
TRIANGULAR STILE
AND POSITION OF
BALL AND DOORS

DISPLAY CABINET

It is essential that the design of a display unit should not dominate the items on display. Unless the unit is consciously being designed in a style that reflects the contents it is best to keep it simple. The size, layout and construction of the unit will depend on the objects to be displayed, which will determine the frequency and placing of the shelves.

There are also environmental requirements which may be necessary, such as the control of moisture, temperature and humidity. Also consider whether you want internal lighting. Some objects may need to be protected with a cover either to keep the dust off or to guard against damage. All these factors will determine the final design and will establish whether your cabinet will be a free standing cabinet, sited against a wall or wall-mounted.

This project piece is wall-mounted and has been designed for displaying a collection of small *objects d'art*. The design can easily be adapted to different sizes.

MAKING SEQUENCE

1. The initial construction consists of a wall-mounted frame with a sheet of ply set into a groove. You can either mortise and tenon joints or mitre the corner (Fig. 1).

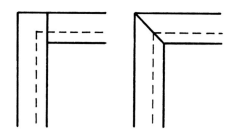

Fig. 1   Wall-mounted frame

2. With that structure complete, make the mounting battens and fit the top one into the frame with glue and screws. The other one will be fixed to the wall. You can secure the cabinet by putting a couple of screws through the front face into the batten (Fig. 2).

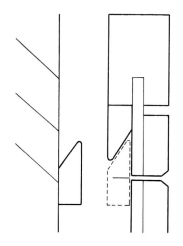

Fig. 2   Mounting battens

3. Make the horizontal slats and fix them carefully and accurately into place with glue and screws from the back. You may want to use natural timber, apply a paint finish or cover them with fabric. Note that the glazed front will fit around all four edges (Fig. 3).

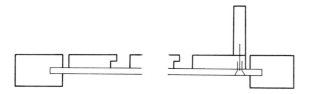

Fig. 3 Fixing horizontal slats

4. When the horizontal slats are in position, make the shelves. The lip on the shelf back could be added to the back top face, or it could be a complete lipping of the back of the shelf. Note the wedge underneath the shelf which ensures that it stays in position. Check that all your shelves fit in the slots and finally plane the support wedges to fit (Fig. 4). There is also a lower fitted shelf, glued and screwed into place from behind (shown in Fig. 3).

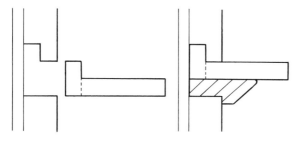

Fig. 4 Making the shelves

5. You now need to make the front glazed cover. You can either use thermoplastic clear sheet material and curve it to fit in place as described in the Tip opposite, or make a timber frame as shown in the main photograph in which the glazing can rest (Fig. 5). It is not advisable to use glass, because of its weight and the difficulty in fixing it. Instead, use one of the highly transparent plastic sheets, either Perspex or Orreglass

(acrylic), which are as clear as glass. They can be cut and drilled with simple tools and bent to shape.

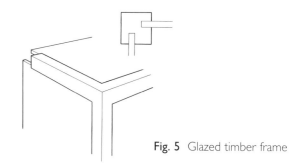

Fig. 5 Glazed timber frame

6. Note how the glazing fits securely into the frame and can be held at the top with the button fitting (Fig. 6a), while the bottom can be fixed to the underneath of the fitted lower shelf (Fig. 6b).

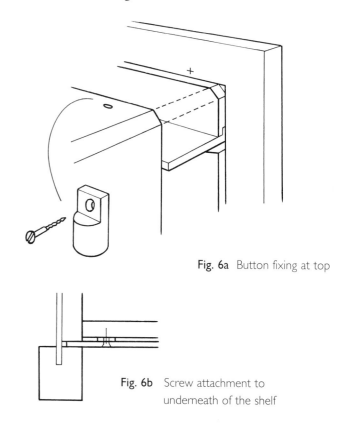

Fig. 6a Button fixing at top

Fig. 6b Screw attachment to underneath of the shelf

TIP

FABRICATING AND BENDING PLASTIC SHEET

First, remove the corners (Fig. 7a). It is then necessary to bend the four sides at right angles to the face. Acrylic sheet can be softened by applying heat (NOT a naked flame – use a hot-air paint stripper) to the area to be bent (Fig. 7b). Do this with care, and you will feel when the plastic has softened enough for it to bend to the required position (Fig. 7c). There are solvents available which allow the material to be joined to itself, so fit plastic slips to the four corners (Fig. 7d).

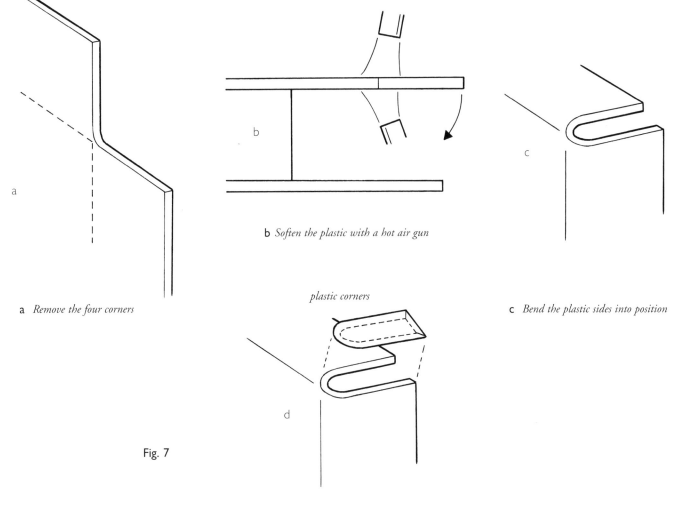

b *Soften the plastic with a hot air gun*

a *Remove the four corners*

c *Bend the plastic sides into position*

plastic corners

Fig. 7

d *Insert plastic slips into the corners*

FITTINGS

Screws

Screws are the commonest fittings and there are two major types. The traditional screw has approximately one third shank and two thirds screw thread.

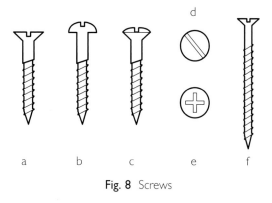

Fig. 8 Screws

You therefore order these screws by length, gauge and type of head. The commonest types of head are countersunk (Fig. 8a), round (Fig. 8b) and raised (Fig. 8c), and the screws turn by two types of screwdriver, a simple slot (Fig. 8d) and a cross head (Fig. 8e). The other type of screw, which is becoming more common is the double spiral screw where the thread takes up most of the length of the screw and the shank is smaller than the thread (Fig. 8f). These screws generally have cross heads. Whenever you are fitting screws, it is good practice to drill a small pilot hole for the thread and a clearance hole for the shank, particularly when using hardwood. When using brass screws, always insert and remove a steel screw of the same size first as the softness of brass will result in screws snapping if the hole has not been pre-threaded. It is also a good idea to lubricate the screw with candlewax or petroleum jelly.

Pins and nails (Fig. 9)

The furniture-maker seldom uses nails, but will often make use of small panel pins, or for even finer work, the similar but thinner veneer pins. When using nails or pins you need a nail punch so that the head can be lost under the timber surface.

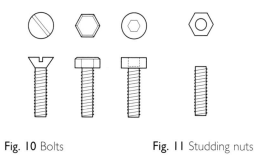

Fig. 9 Nails

Bolts

There are many occasions when a bolt or machine screw will be useful. Bolts are produced with a range of threads and heads such as countersunk, hexagonal or allen key heads (Fig. 10).

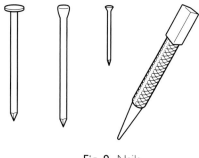

Fig. 10 Bolts   **Fig. 11** Studding nuts

It is possible to make your own bolts by using threaded studding and nuts (Fig. 11a) (available in different thread sizes). This can be used in combination with the 'T' nut (see Fig. 11b). An alternative is the to use threaded inserts which are set in the wood (Fig. 11c).

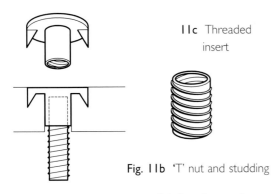

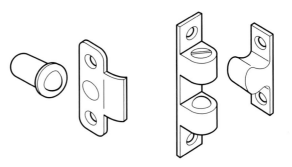

11c Threaded insert

Fig. 11b 'T' nut and studding

Fig. 13 Ball catches

The barrel nut (Fig. 12a) is useful for fixing frames to avoid timber jointing. Use lengths of studding with threaded end caps to give a joint with neat fixings on both faces (Fig. 12b).

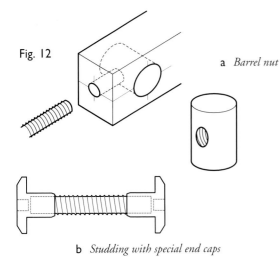

Fig. 12

a *Barrel nut*

b *Studding with special end caps*

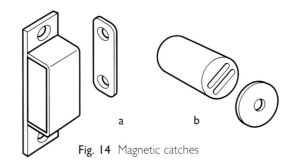

a   **b**

Fig. 14 Magnetic catches

There is a knock down system based on a cam action (see Fig. 15), which is useful if you want furniture which will dismantle.

Door catches

For doors and flaps, there is a range of closing fittings available. The ball catch is widely used and its simplest construction is a round barrel and a sprung ball (Fig. 13a). You could also use a fitting where the two balls are adjustable (Fig. 13b). Another option is the magnetic catch either using magnets that fit on the surface (Fig. 14a) , or the compact barrel magnetic catch (Fig. 14).

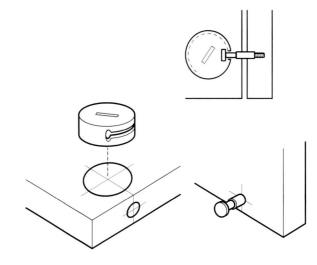

Fig. 15 Cam action system

There are proprietary fittings for joining cabinets together and the plastic blocks shown here are a common example – they screw to two components and are then joined with a bolt (see Fig. 16).

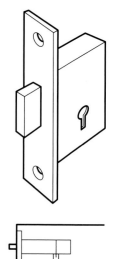

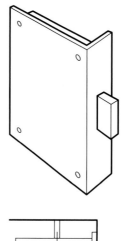

a *Cabinet lock fitted to the inside face*   b *Mortise lock fits into mortise in edge of door*

Fig. 17 Locks

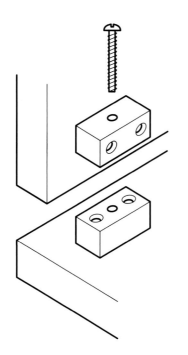

Fig. 16 Plastic blocks screwed to inside of cabinet

Of the wide range of locks available, a cabinet lock is fixed on the inside face of doors or a mortise lock fits into a mortise inside the door (Fig. 17a and b). When making doors that open like a Fall front you can attach stays which hold this fall at a 90-degree angle (Fig. 18).

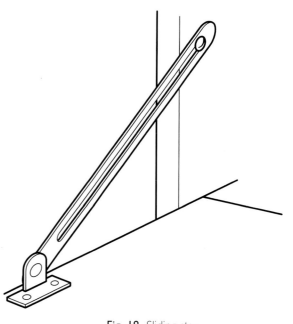

Fig. 18 Sliding stay

CUSTOMIZING

The very nature of a display cabinet requires it to be neutral and to display the objects within to the maximum effect. Some of the customizing of this piece does not therefore seek to change substantially the appearance of the piece, but to change small details so that it will sit more readily in the position you have chosen for it. The main suggested alteration are to the glazing detail, the back surface of the display area and the nature of the shelves. The piece as shown was made in the modern style.

COUNTRY

This style should be in light timbers and this could be a version where the glazing would be suitable for a frame approach rather than a plastic 'box'. The framework is of timber, but it is advisable for the glazing to remain in plastic since this can be drilled and screwed and/or glued into place; this makes it easy to fit the front using the same method as in the worked example. Notice in the drawing the careful rounding of the corners/edges of the glazing frame and the main backboard. The display surface could be hessian or

'Japanese' wallpaper, but always decide this finish with reference to the items to be displayed. For the shelves, timber is ideal to match the structure.

REPRODUCTION

As with the other items, this will require a dark timber for the backboard. A glazed timber frame has been used for this version. Using a fabric for the display surface would look good, as would either timber or glass for the shelves.

DESIGNER

This option departs from the two glazing details suggested above. Instead of making a plastic box or a timber frame, you could purchase a plastic dome (or bubble) such as is used for roof lights. This would dictate the size and shape of the main backboards and the shelves. The fixing would probably have to be from the front, since these units are generally vacuum formed and the edges are flat. The main backboard could still be of timber, but you could try a metallic finish for the display surface and metal or glass for the shelves.

MATERIALS LIST: DISPLAY CABINET (NOMINAL SIZES: IN/MM)

Item	Quantity	Length	Width	Thickness
Frame stiles (solid timber)	2	25 in / 620 mm	1½ in / 40 mm	1⅛ in / 30 mm
Frame rails (solid timber)	2	15 in / 370 mm	1½ in / 40 mm	1⅛ in / 30 mm
Plywood panel (cut to fit grooves in frame)	1	23 in / 540 mm	12 in / 290 mm	¼ in / 6 mm
Fixed support batten	1	12 in / 300 mm	⅞ in / 22 mm	⁷⁄₁₆ in / 12 mm
Wall-mounted support batten	1	12 in / 255 mm	1½ in / 40 mm	⁷⁄₁₆ in / 12 mm
Fixed lower shelf (solid timber)	1	10 in / 255 mm	3¼ in / 80 mm	¾ in / 18 mm
Horizontal slats (timber or ply, face finished)	5	11 in / 270 mm	3¹¹⁄₁₆ in / 91 mm	⁷⁄₁₆ in / 12 mm
Shelves (timber or glass)	4	10 in / 255 mm	3¼ in / 80 mm	⁵⁄₁₆ in / 8 mm
Shelf support wedges	4	10 in / 255 mm	1³⁄₁₆ in / 35 mm	⅜ / 10 mm
Front glazed cover (either thermoplastic [acrylic or polycarbonate] for bending to shape shown)	1	30 in / 760 mm	21 in / 500 mm	¼ / 6 mm
or glazed timber frame				
(clear sheets to make front cover, in timber frame, with either clear plastic or glass)	1 (front) 2 (sides) 1 (top) 2	21 in / 520 mm 21 in / 520 mm 11 in / 270 mm 11 in / 270 mm	11 in / 270 mm 4 in / 100 mm 4 in / 100 mm 4 in / 100 mm	¼ in / 6 mm ¼ in / 6 mm ¼ in / 6 mm ¼ in / 6 mm
timber frame to make front glazed cover, sections machined to L-section, cut 2 stiles, 2 rails & 4 corners from length	1	8 in	¾ in / 20 mm	¾ in / 20 mm

Please note that the measurements shown in imperial and metric on the working drawings are not direct conversions of each other, but are adapted to make each set clear.

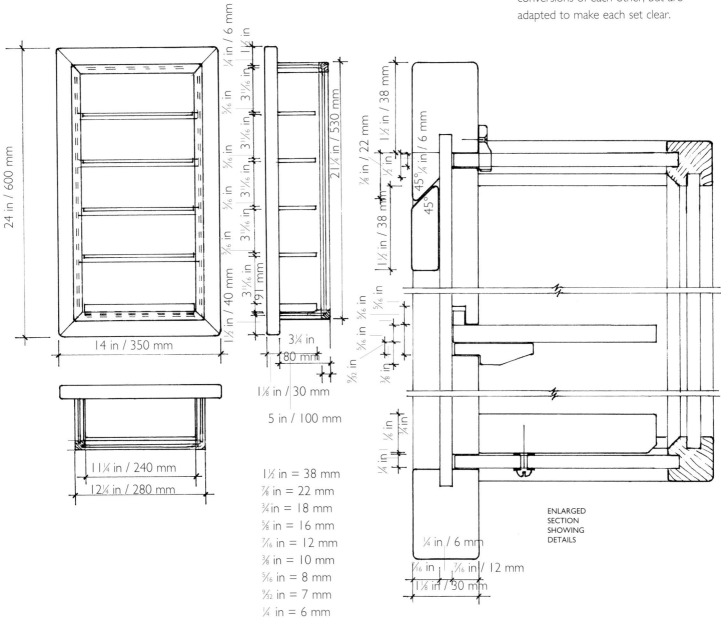

1½ in = 38 mm
⅞ in = 22 mm
¾ in = 18 mm
⅝ in = 16 mm
⁷⁄₁₆ in = 12 mm
⅜ in = 10 mm
⁵⁄₁₆ in = 8 mm
⁹⁄₃₂ in = 7 mm
¼ in = 6 mm
⅛ in = 1 mm

ENLARGED
SECTION
SHOWING
DETAILS

SETTLE

For this particular design a number of tongue and groove boards have been used for the front, back and sides. The basic design aims to offer a comfortable seat with a generous amount of storage space. The drawing shows three different heights for the back and before deciding on the height you will need to decide how you want to use the settle. For use with a table, a low back would be preferable and a high back would look better if the settle is to be placed against a wall. The length can be adapted in the same way to suit your purpose. If the settle is primarily for sitting on, it is worthwhile having a slight rake on the seat to improve comfort.

MAKING SEQUENCE

1. The basis of the design and the first priority is the construction of the two side frames. Each frame is based on four components; a front leg, a back leg, a lower rail and a top rail (Fig. 1). These can be jointed whichever way you prefer, either using mortise and tenons or other joints such as dowels. Note how the front top rail is halved into the upright back leg.

2. When these two frames are completed, make the four longitudinal cross rails and then choose between mechanical fittings or mortise and tenons for the joints. If you use screws or a bolt and a barrel nut, you will be able to construct the piece as you work. If you wish to use mortise and tenons, you will not be able to make a full assembly until near the end.

3. Make the flat back rail and cut it carefully to size and fit it. Then mark, cut and fit the plywood bottom. This will sit on the bottom front and side rails and is notched round the four legs. It should be held in position using screws.

4. Cut the timber boards for the front, back and sides to length following the working drawing and join them together. If you wish to see the ends of the sideboards from the front as shown in Fig. 2a, fix the front and back boards first, then apply the boards to the ends. Work the other way round if you wish the ends of the front boards to show on the sides (Fig. 2b).

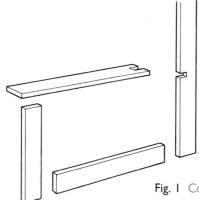

Fig. 1 Components of side frames

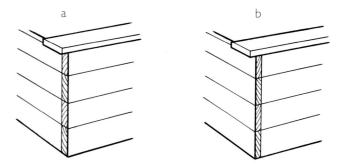

Fig. 2 Applying the timber boards

5. These panels can be fixed in several ways (Fig. 2c). If you use screws, the screw head will remain visible. Similarly, small coach bolts will show the bolt head and a washer. Alternatively, you can use screws and cover them with timber plugs.

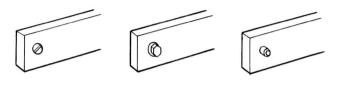

c *Applying the timber boards*

6. Now make the seat, again from boards. This needs to be hinged (see page 86) to form the cover for the storage box. The design shows a cleat (a wood batten fitted across the ends of the boards). For greater strength you can fit battens to the underside – see Tip opposite.

7. Fit the back rails. If you are making the height low, fit the three rails in place as shown to form a comfortable lumbar support (Fig. 3a). It is the only way to achieve comfort in a low back. If you are making the back shoulder or head height you will need to groove the rails on the edges to accept ply panels (Fig. 3b and c). These rails can be fitted with mortise and tenons if you are using that option, or with screws or bolts with barrel nuts.

8. Make the arms (Fig. 4). The shape of both each arm rest and support is optional, although a simple design with a scroll shape works well. Cut the arms out and shape them roughly, then smooth them and fix in position. The support can be tenoned into the side frame and dowelled under the arm as shown. Fix the arm at the rear with a small halving joint and with dowels or screws.

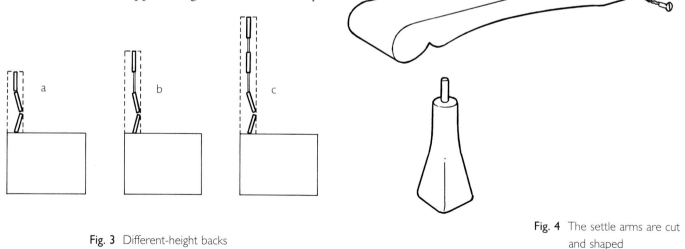

Fig. 4 The settle arms are cut and shaped

Fig. 3 Different-height backs

TIP

JOINING BOARDS

For this piece you will probably have to join a number of boards to make up the width needed. It is often advisable to do this anyway, since unless a board is quarter sawn it is very liable to move. When joining boards together, ensure that the surfaces are planed flat and square (see page 14). You can simply use glue and cramps when assembling, but it is often better to use loose tongues, biscuits or dowels to provide a stronger, edge-to-edge join. When you arrange the boards, try to ensure that the grain direction runs alternately from board to board as shown (Fig.5) to minimize any distortion.

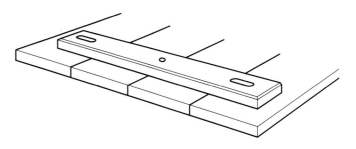

Fig. 6 Support battens fitted underneath

screw while the other screws should be in slots, to allow for cross-grain movement that will occur as a result of changes in the moisture content of the atmosphere (Fig. 7).

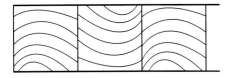

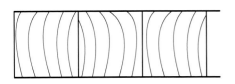

Fig. 5 Arrangement of end grain when joining boards

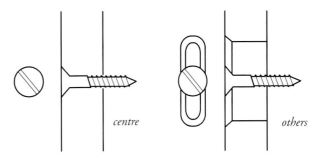

Fig. 7 Methods of screwing battens in place

SHAPED WORK

Furniture-making techniques require precision to create flat surfaces and square dimensions. The approach to shaping wood used in woodturning and woodcarving is much freer.

Whenever large surfaces are made in this way, they will generally need battens underneath to help prevent the board buckling (Fig. 6). However, because of timber movement the centre should be fixed with a normal

After designing and planning the work, it is worthwhile making a mock-up of the shaped pieces by carving foam plastic blocks such as polystyrene or polyurethane before working on the actual timber. This would be particularly helpful in the case of the arm of the settle. When you are ready to start on the final component, use a square or rectangular block of timber. You can remove most of the waste by sawing with power or machine tools. The process of band sawing a shaped chair arm is illustrated here. The cuts are made on both faces but not completed until the very end so that there is always an intact block on which to work (Figs 8 and 9).

When you are sawing by hand, use a coping or bow saw. With power tools, use a jigsaw or fret saw and with machine tools a band saw. Having removed the bulk by sawing, you can then shape and smooth using gouges, rasps, files and special curved rasp files called rifflers. For very complex work sanding may have to be carried out by hand using sandpaper, although a disc sander or the end of the belt sander may be appropriate for less fine work.

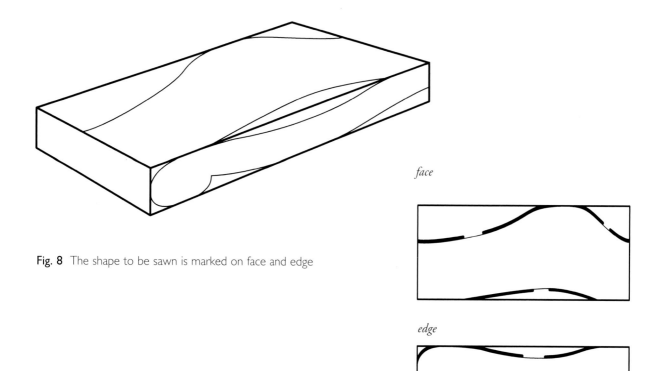

Fig. 8 The shape to be sawn is marked on face and edge

face

edge

Fig. 9 Safe cutting when making curved shapes. Saw where the lines are heavy and finally make the short cuts by hand

CUSTOMIZING

The project was made in the country style using natural timber planks on a structural frame.

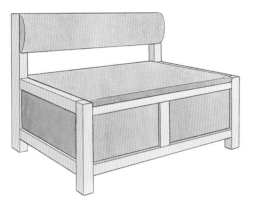

MODERN

This version makes use of the basic structural frame with panels fitted within it. Depending upon the length required, there will be a need for some vertical divisions in the front and back, partly for structural reasons and partly to give a good visual balance. The panel is of plywood and can either be fitted into grooves on assembly or fitted into rebates on completion of the main structure. The seat and the back can be upholstered or have loose cushions.

REPRODUCTION

This could use a framed approach, the storage chest being emphasized and using panels in frames, with a plinth and overhanging top. In the period in which this construction is found oak was generally used as the main timber. The back can also use similar panels.

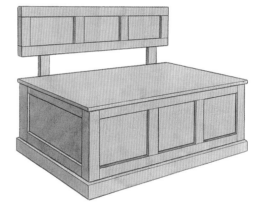

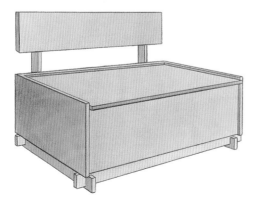

DESIGNER

This approach is based on a panel construction, the main structural frames being made from solid timber and the sides, back, front and seat made from manufactured board. You can apply colours and textures to achieve an interesting effect.

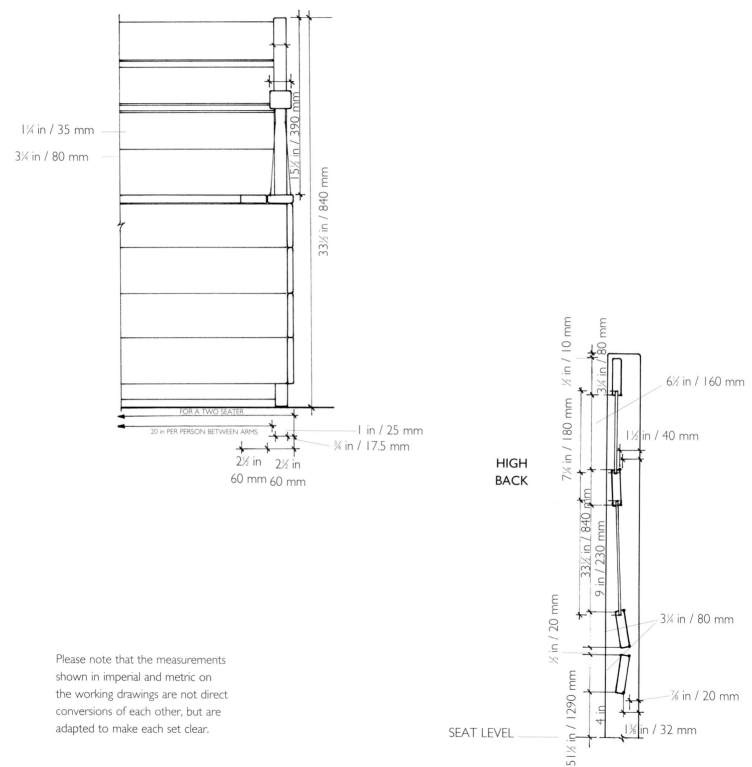

1¼ in / 35 mm

3¼ in / 80 mm

15½ in / 390 mm

33½ in / 840 mm

FOR A TWO SEATER

20 in PER PERSON BETWEEN ARMS

1 in / 25 mm

¾ in / 17.5 mm

2½ in

2½ in

60 mm 60 mm

Please note that the measurements
shown in imperial and metric on
the working drawings are not direct
conversions of each other, but are
adapted to make each set clear.

HIGH
BACK

½ in / 10 mm

¾ in / 80 mm

6½ in / 160 mm

1½ in / 40 mm

7¼ in / 180 mm

33½ in / 840 mm

9 in / 230 mm

3¼ in / 80 mm

½ in / 20 mm

⅞ in / 20 mm

1⅜ in / 32 mm

4 in

SEAT LEVEL

51½ in / 1290 mm

TOTAL HT.

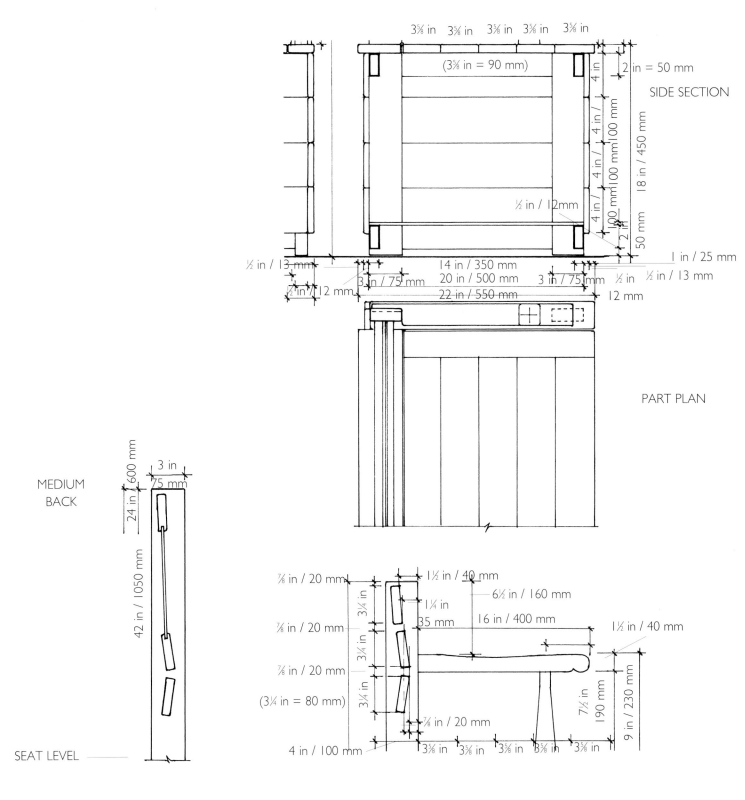

SIDE SECTION

PART PLAN

MEDIUM
BACK

SEAT LEVEL

MATERIALS LIST: SETTLE (NOMINAL SIZES: IN/MM)

The following sizes are given for low back version as per drawing (from seat height 15 ½ in or 370 mm). If you wish to make medium (24 in or 600 mm) & high backs (33 ½ in or 840 mm), see details and extend the length of the back accordingly. These lengths are measured from the seat dimension.

Item	*Quantity*	*Length*	*Width*	*Thickness*
Main structure, back legs (for 2 side frames)	2	34 in / 850 mm	3 in / 75 mm	1 in / 25 mm
Main structure, front legs (for 2 side frames)	2	18 in / 450 mm	3 in / 75 mm	1 in / 25 mm
Main structure, front to back rails (for 2 side frames)	4	20 in / 500 mm	2 in / 50 mm	1 in / 25 mm
Main structure (front to back top flat rails)	2	22 in / 550 mm	2½ in / 60 mm	⅞ in / 20 mm
Main structure, cross rails between sides	4	451 in / 1120 mm	2 in / 50 mm	1 in / 25 mm
Plywood base fitted inside main structure	1	43½ in / 1,1085 mm	20 in / 500 mm	¼ in / 6 mm
Matchboard (for front & back cladding)	8	45 in / 1120 mm	4 in / 100 mm	½in / 12 mm
Matchboard (for cladding on 2 sides. Decide if you want front or sides to overlap)	8	22 in / 550 mm	4 in / 100 mm	½in / 12 mm
Rear side to side back top flat rail	1	40 in / 1000 mm	4 / 100 mm	⅞ / 20 mm
Matchboard for seat/ hinged opening top, side to side	5	36 in / 900 mm	3⅝ in / 90 mm	⅞ in / 20 mm
Cleats for end of seat	2	18 in / 460 mm	2½ in / 60 mm	⅞ in / 20 mm
Arms	2	18 in / 460 mm	2 in / 50 mm	1½ in /40 mm
Arm supports	2	10 in / 250 mm	2 in / 50 mm	2 in / 50 mm
Horizontal slats for low back	3	45 in / 1120 mm	3¼ in / 80 mm	⅞ in / 20 mm
Option 1 Ply panel for medium back (to fit in grooves in 2 top rails)	1	43½ in / 1085 mm	9¾ in / 250 mm	¼ in / 6 mm
Option 2 Ply extra panel for high back (1 extra rail, needed)	1	43½ in / 1085 mm	7¼ in / 180 mm	¼in / 6 mm
Extra rail	1	45 in / 1120 mm	3¼ in / 80 mm	⅞in / 20 mm

LIST OF SUPPLIERS

General Supplies
Large DIY retail 'sheds', such as **Homebase**, **Do-It-All**, **Wickes** and **Jewson**, are a useful first point of call. Alternatively, small local hardware shops will generally give good service and advice.

Furniture Fittings
Trade suppliers will often only supply in bulk, but they sometimes will have local retail outlets.

Hafele
Swift Valley Industrial Estate
Rugby
Warwickshire CV21 1RD
Tel: 01788 542020

Timber
The sheds mentioned above will stock softwoods and some manufactured board, but quality hardwoods are more difficult. The following may supply mail order, or look in the Yellow Pages under 'Timber Merchants':

John Boddy Timber Ltd
Riverside Sawmills
Boroughbridge
North Yorkshire YO5 9LJ
Tel: 01423 322370

Interesting Timbers
Hazel Farm
Compton Martin
Somerset BS18 6LH
Tel: 01761 463356

North Heigham Sawmills Ltd
Paddock Street
Norwich NR2 4TW
Tel: 01603 622978

Veneers
Capital Veneer Co Ltd
Unit 12
Bow Industrial Estate
Carpenters Road
London
Stratford E15 2DZ
Tel: 0181 525 0300

Crispin J. & Sons
92-96 Curtain Road
London EC2A 3AA
Tel: 0171 739 4857

C.B. Veneer Ltd
Progress Road
Sands Industrial Estate
High Wycombe
Buckinghamshire
Tel: 01494 471959

Tools
Axminster Power Tools Centre
Chard Street
Axminster
Devon EX13 5DZ
Tel: 01297 33535

T Brooker & Sons Ltd
39 Bucklersbury
Hitchin
Hertfordshire SG5 1BQ
Tel: 01462 434501

Murray's Tool Store
83 Morrison Street
Edinburgh EH3 8BU
Tel: 0131 229 1577

WJT Crafts and Woodturning Supplies
New Farm Road Industrial Estate
Prospect Road
New Alresford
Hampshire SO24 9QF
Tel: 01962 735411

Brassware
Martin and Company
97 Camden Street
Birmingham B1 3DG
Tel: 0121 233 2111

John Lawrence and Co (Dover) Ltd
Granville Street
Dover
Kent CT16 2LF
Tel: 01304 201425

Router Cutters
Trend Machinery and Cutting Tools Ltd
Unit 'N' Penfold Works
Imperial Way
Watford
Hertfordshire WD2 4YF
Tel: 01923 249911

Cabinetmakers' Supplies
Fiddes and Son
Florence Works
Brindley Road
Cardiff CF1 7TX
Tel: 01222 340323

USA

Timber
Maurice L Condon Co Inc.
248 Ferris Avenue
White Plains NY 10603

Tools
Frog Tool Co Ltd
700 W Jackson Boulevard
Chicago, IL 60606

Garrett Wade Company
161 Avenue of the Americas
New York, NY 10013

Woodcraft Supply Corp.
41 Atlantic Avenue
Box 4000
Woburn, MA 01888
(also hinges, brassware, fiber rush, finishing materials)

Finishing Supplies
Mohawk Finishing Products Inc.
State Highway 30
Amsterdam, NY 12010

Brassware
Ball and Ball
463 West Lincoln Highway
Exton, PA 19341

INDEX

A
abrasives 45
adhesives 32
adjustable shelf supports 39, 40
assembling triangular
    shapes 103

B
basic preparation 14
bending plastic sheet 111
biscuit jointer 12
bits 12
bookcase 36–49
brace 12
bradawl 12
butt hinges, fitting 63, 64

C
chisels 12
Corner Cupboard 92–99
cramps
    G-cramp 13
    sash 13
    web/band 13
cramping frames 22

D
Display Cabinet 108–117
drawers 70, 71
drills 12
Drop-leaf Table 84–91

E
equipment 10

F
finishing 13, 78, 79, 80
fittings 112
    screws 112
    pins and nails 112
    bolts 112
    door catches 113
    locks 114
frame construction and jointing
    24, 25

G
gauges, marking 10
gouges 12
grinder 13

H
halving joint, cutting 28
hammer 12
hardwoods 31
Hi-fi Unit 76–83

J
joining boards 121
jointing 12

K
knock-down fittings 113, 114

M
Magazine Rack 50–57
mallet 12
manufactured board 72
marking and measuring
    tools 10

marking out 16, 17
Mirror/Picture Frame 20–27
mitres, cutting 20

O
Occasional Table 28– 35
oilstone 13

P
planes, hand, electric and
    machine 10, 12
planing straight and square 15
plastic sheet, fabricating and
    bending 111

R
router 12
rules, folding, steel and metal
    tape 10

S
saws
    for curves, keyhole, coping,
        bow 11
    hand, crosscut, ripsaw, panel,
        tenon, dovetail 10, 11
    machine and hand powered
        10, 11
scraper plane 13
scrapers 13, 44
screwdriver 12
seasoning 32
Settle 118–126
Sewing Box 100–107
shaped work 121, 122

sharpening
    edge tools 43
    grinder 13
    oilstone 13
softwoods 31
spokeshave 12
squares, try square and sliding
    bevel 10
surfacing tools 10

T
tenons, sawing 87
timber
    carcass construction 61
    choosing 41
    colour, pattern and
        texture 53
    preparing 14
    softwoods and
        hardwoods 41, 42
    solid 31
tongues 22
TV and Video Unit 68–75

V
veneer 95, 96

W
Wall-hung Cabinet 58–67
wheelbrace 12